Marry a FRIEND

Finding Someone to Marry Who Is Truly Right for You

Counsel and encouragement for Christians—and for anyone seeking a partner for marriage

M. Blaine Smith

SilverCrest
B•O•O•K•S

SilverCrest Books
P.O. Box 448
Damascus, Maryland 20872

e-mail: scr@nehemiahministries.com
www.nehemiahministries.com

ISBN: 978-0-9840322-0-4

Library of Congress Control Number: 2011917052

Table of Contents

Some names and minor details in stories have been changed, to protect the identities of those involved.

Part One

* * * * * * * * * *

Rethinking Your
Perfect Mate

One

* * * * * * * * * *

An Achievable Dream!

THE DREAM OF A LIFETIME RELATIONSHIP! CHANCES are good, since you've picked up this book, that this is your single greatest longing. It certainly was for me as a young single man. And most singles whom I talk with admit that the hope for a good marriage is their most burning aspiration—far ahead of anything that's in second place.

In generations past, most who wanted to be married enjoyed vastly greater family and social support in finding a spouse. Most married young and, compared with challenges today, suffered minimal struggle in finding a mate. Times, of course, have changed, and they have changed drastically; today most of us largely have to fend for ourselves in seeking to fulfill this greatest of our life's dreams.

Even with today's challenges, some do have the good fortune of finding marriage almost effortlessly. A serious relationship develops spontaneously with a friend or acquaintance while they're young, moves naturally to marriage, and they truly do live happily ever after. Yes, it happens.

But not frequently—even though such examples stand out and catch our attention, and too often become the ideal for how we imagine our own journey to marriage should take place. Yet in reality, most of us in America today suffer plenty of struggle and disappointment in searching for a spouse, and the process takes years for many people.

The Challenge for Women

My role as a Christian teacher and counselor brings me into contact most frequently with Christian singles and the special challenges they face in finding someone to marry. If you're not a Christian, or aren't certain, please don't put this book down. You'll find most of its discussion relevant to your own search for marriage, I promise you. But I want to begin by addressing Christians specifically, for so many of them tell me they are deeply frustrated in seeking marriage, and I intend this book especially to address their needs and concerns.

Arlene, whom I met this past week when speaking to a Christian singles group in Washington, is a good example. My topic was the importance of pursuing your personal dreams, and it spurred her to speak with me afterwards. Arlene told me she has long been discouraged about being single, and asked how she might put her dream of getting married on the front burner. She's in her mid-forties now and rarely gets asked out, she explained. She fears the opportunity to marry may have eluded her for good. Men just aren't taking initiative, and she wonders if she can do anything to improve her prospects.

Several things were striking to me about Arlene and her predicament. She is attractive, vivacious, bright, and clearly a big-hearted person. In addition, she works at the White House—one of the most prestigious workplaces in our city, and one where many other singles are employed. It is, in short, a better job setting than most for her to meet someone, and the Washington area in general offers outstanding opportunities. On top of that, she belongs to a large, dynamic church that many singles of all ages attend.

Yet in spite of these strong advantages, she isn't dating, and doesn't see anything obvious she can do to improve her options. She did try a popular online service for a few months, but unsuccessfully, and she was uncomfortable with its anonymous approach to getting acquainted. The situation is no different for many of her Christian female friends, she added, who have so much to offer the right man, but aren't getting noticed, and seem destined to stay single for ever.

Arlene and her friends could be postcard children for countless Christian women today. So many I speak with would dearly love to be married, and are so ready for marriage and have so much to offer, that they are overqualified, if anything. Yet they're at their wit's end about how to find someone suitable. Many, like Arlene and her friends, are in churches and social settings where they have plenty of opportunity to meet single Christian men in their age range. Yet these men might as well be on another planet as far as these women are concerned—for as year drifts into year, none are showing romantic interest in them.

Arlene voiced a further frustration, which gets to the heart of the problem for so many women: She feels there is little she can do *as a woman* to initiate a relationship. It's the man's responsibility to show initial interest, and then to take the first steps toward getting a relationship in motion. It would be so much easier if she were free to do more initiating at these early stages of getting acquainted and dating.

I find that most single women, whether Christian or not, share Arlene's frustration. They may be strong self-initiators in other areas, like education and career. Yet they feel their hands are tied when it comes to launching a relationship. And so their frustration is compounded: not only is their love life without momentum, but they feel helpless to change things. Singleness is like a prison, where their only hope is that some man may care enough to pardon them.

While the fear of never marrying is felt acutely by many single women as they pass into their thirties and beyond, a surprising number of younger woman carry a similar sinking feeling that their options are running out, and they feel powerless to change their destiny. I recall a long chat with a woman who deeply wanted to be married yet feared the opportunity had passed her by. Many of her friends had married, and the one relationship that held hope for her had ended. She wondered if God was indicating through it all that she should abandon her hope of marrying and set her heart on staying single. She was twenty-two.

The Challenge for Men

But here's the biggest surprise—at least for women who think that men hold all the cards in seeking marriage: A surprising number of men are just as frustrated in their search, and feel just as powerless to do what is needed to spark a serious relationship. And I mean wonderful, well-qualified men. In my years of ministering with singles, I'm certain as many men as women have confessed to me that they have no dating life, and that marriage seems forever the impossible dream.

I've known countless single men who would make terrific husbands and fathers, but, lacking confidence, rarely date at all. Many are simply shy; they're so traumatized over the possibility of rejection, that they never take the first steps to break the ice with women who interest them, even though they dream about doing it a lot.

Others aren't as phobic about rejection, yet still are stymied by assumptions of failure. They always conclude that someone they want to ask out won't be interested, so they don't bother to try at all. Negative thinking keeps them stuck in their inertia, even in the face of opportunities where they would, in fact, succeed.

For many others, the main problem is a lack of focus and know-how. Some have concentrated so strongly on their education and career that their relationship life has never had a chance to blossom. These men may be brilliant professionally and highly successful. Yet their social life hasn't kept pace, and they've never been coached on the most basic points of dating. Some feel awkward even striking up a conversation with a woman who attracts them romantically, let alone asking her out. And some Christian men are uncertain if they *should* take initiative, even in the face of an obvious opportunity, or just leave it to the Lord to bring about marriage for them in his own way and time.

Just recently, a college student e-mailed me, asking my advice. A woman he has liked for some time has broken up with her boyfriend, he explained. He then asked me two questions: Is it worth the risk to ask her out? And, if so, how should he go about developing a relationship with her?

Most interesting is that he was asking *me*, a total stranger, for this counsel—apparently uncertain where else to turn for it, or embarrassed to admit to his friends that he needs this Dating 101 advice. You would be surprised how many men of all ages have asked such questions of me, and how many are held back by such a lack of basic know-how.

Running the Race but Never Winning

Countless women and men who are eager for marriage long for some momentum toward their dream. Their relationship life is at a standstill, and they don't know how to get it moving. For them, just to gain a serious dating relationship would be a gigantic step forward.

Many others are at the opposite extreme. They have plenty of momentum in their relationship life, even abundant opportunity to date, but none of it is leading to marriage. Some bounce from one dead-end relationship to another, while others enjoy a number of promising relationships that in the end never progress to marriage.

Others are more at a mid-point in their relationship search. They refuse to sit with their hands tied waiting for their prince or princess to come, and they take plenty of initiative—but it rarely succeeds. Some men are not at all shy and will ask a woman out at any opportunity, but for various reasons usually get turned down. If they do get the date, they seldom get a second or third, and their hope for a real relationship is constantly disappointed.

While some do succeed stunningly with Internet dating services, many fall into a rut with them. Some rarely get beyond exchanging e-mail with their online contacts, yet they try and try again. One woman I know has been "closed" more than 150 times at this stage, yet she continues to take the same basic approach, hoping it will eventually work for her.

It's especially easy with online services to fall into self-defeating patterns that you never recognize nor correct. If you make an obvious blunder in real-life socializing, it's always possible a friend will notice and care enough to point it out to you. But because you pursue online connecting in private, no one is there to spontaneously offer such coaching. And the extreme convenience of the Internet, and the ease of making initial contacts (vastly simpler than getting dressed up, traveling to a social event, and mingling for hours—instead just log on anytime 24/7!), can leave you vulnerable to repeating the same unproductive patterns over and over.

What if God Wants Me to Stay Single?
People are hindered and frustrated in their search for a spouse for many different reasons. But one thing Christians share in common is confusion over what God is saying through it all. Most begin to wonder at some point if their failure to find someone to marry means God wants them to let go of their hope for marriage and set their heart on staying single.

A thoughtful Christian man, Mike, asked me this question recently, and if anyone has the right to ask it, he does! At 48, he has been through more promising relationships than he can count. "In the last one," he explained, "the woman told me that I have every manly quality she is looking for; she also praised me to her friends, and they told me so! Yet she just couldn't get her heart to tell her, 'Yes, marry this fellow.' I was extremely disappointed once again."

This led him to ask me what God may be indicating through these repeated failures. "Could he be telling me that marriage just isn't in his plan for me? But then why this incredible desire? Or could he be telling me to wait? But what if God is saying no? If he is, I swear it would be disappointing, but it would also be an incredible relief knowing this. Then, rather than concentrate my prayers on asking him to bless me and show me his will, I would concentrate on asking him to give me the peace and strength to accept reality and take a new direction. And possibly at that point I could change my life and thinking so as not to dwell on this hope daily."

Mike's concern with God's will at this point in his experience is *so* understandable, and he couldn't possibly have raised the question in a more reverent and thoughtful way. The problem, though, is that once you even start musing about this, finding the heart to continue searching for a spouse becomes more difficult—and Mike's motivation is clearly wearing thin.

If you truly want to be married, God never wants you to conclude that he wills for you to stay permanently single, no matter how many disappointments you experience. The proper question to ask in the face of repeated failures isn't "does God want me to quit?"—but *"why are these setbacks occurring?"* When you look carefully, you often find that, without realizing it, you're doing certain things that are sabotaging good opportunities. By changing your attitude and approach in certain ways, your chances for success greatly improve when you try again.

It's here that modern Christian teaching often makes it very difficult for the single Christian. The notion that God may be calling you to remain single even though you want to be married, is often taught in singles literature and proclaimed by Christian teachers and preachers. More often than not, it's the prevailing philosophy in singles ministries, both within churches and without. And it's too often the advice given to lonely and discouraged singles who seek counsel and encouragement from Christian leaders and friends.

While such counsel is usually well-intentioned, it misses the heart of biblical thinking drastically, as I'll stress below. And it's a major reason why the search for a marriage partner often is more difficult for the Christian than it is for others.

The Goal of This Book

It should be just the opposite! We have the power of Christ within us and the guidance of God in our lives. And we have abundant evidence in Scripture that God wills for most people to marry, and extends special help to those who draw upon it in seeking a partner for life.

For the longest time, I've wanted to write a book giving encour-agement and direction to those who seriously want to find someone to marry. A previous book of mine, *Should I Get Married?*, helps you decide whether to marry once you are in a serious relationship. This current book provides much more of a map for finding that relationship in the first place. As in that earlier book, I'll stress that friendship, more than romance, provides the best basis for a happy, healthy, enduring marriage. Yet I'll look closely at how appreciat-ing this principle is stunningly helpful in looking for the right per-son—sometimes simplifying your search considerably. It can keep you from spinning your wheels in a dead-end relationship, or from wasting time pursuing an enticing relationship that just isn't right for you. And it increases the chance you'll see the treasure in some-one you might be overlooking.

While I'll look at this friendship factor from many angles in this book, I'll also offer much practical guidance about how to find a special friend to marry. We who long to be married need abundant practical advice about how to get off ground zero and proceed with our search in a manner that is both honoring to God and productive. I'll offer the best counsel I possibly can on all the how-tos, in order to point you toward steps that will help you succeed. I won't be suggesting a "one size fits all" strategy, I assure you, but will help you determine approaches that are right *for you*, in light of who you are and the circumstances in which you find yourself. While online dating services may work well for friends of yours, for instance, you may do better to invest your time in certain social activities, and to seek a relationship there.

We who are looking for a spouse also need motivation—and we need it desperately. The single greatest deterrent to finding someone to marry is discouragement. It's tragically easy to lose the heart to continue the search for a mate—which almost always will succeed if you persist enough. So I'll do everything I can to boost your optimism about succeeding. I'll look also at the importance of simply *wanting* to be married, and at what you can do to keep your desire to marry strong—for insufficient desire can keep you stuck in the inertia of singleness, even when you would be truly happier married. I'll provide as much encouragement as I can throughout this book to stay in the fight—strongly believing that with the right spirit and approach you will succeed!

That conviction is fueled by the examples of countless people I've known during four decades of ministering to singles who have found outstanding marriages, many at points where they were tempted to give up hope. And it's fueled by abundant evidence in Scripture that God is on our side as we seek a mate, and that we have strong reason to expect success if we take proper responsibility and move forward in faith.

Moving Ahead

I'll never forget the exuberant comment a woman I once counseled made repeatedly to me. Nancy was engaged, and astounded at her good fortune, for she had suffered disappointment in several previous relationships. She had nearly lost hope that God intended her ever to marry, but now at 33 had found Nathan. And over and over she exclaimed, "I just can't believe that God has preserved this wonderful man for me!"

Nathan, as I discovered—this man who was so well-preserved—had enjoyed only one brief relationship in college, and since had scarcely dated at all. Yet at 35, he was mature, deep, and caring, and a perfect match for Nancy—who had every right to be so jubilant over God's extraordinary provision.

If you've long wished to be married but have lost your hope, it's time to revive it! Let Nathan and Nancy's example inspire you as you move into this study, along with many other encouraging examples we'll look at in the pages ahead. And it's my sincerest hope that the day will come for you—and sooner than you expect—when you also will say with stunned gratitude, "I just can't believe God has preserved this wonderful person for me!" That, my friend, is a most reasonable hope and goal for you to embrace—for above all else, God's hand in your life is not shortened (Is 59:1).

Two

* * * * * * * * * *

The Friendship Path to Marriage

BEFORE DOING ANYTHING ELSE, I WANT TO TRY TO EX-
pand your thinking a bit about how marriage might come about for
you. If you're discouraged in your search for someone to marry,
and believe your chance for success isn't good, it may be because
you're thinking too narrowly about your options. Most people assume that good marriages always result from the same familiar process: romance ignites between a woman and a man, and they are
swept into marriage on the winds of it. And, yes, no question that
many good marriages do occur this way.

Yet an astounding number of them spring from strong friendships, where often romance isn't even a factor at first. While romantic feelings come as the relationship develops, friendship continues
to energize it more than romance. If you'll look around you and ask
the right questions, you'll probably be surprised to find that many
of the marriages you most admire have resulted this way.

While the friendship path to marriage holds the greatest promise
for many, it is rarely articulated well by those who teach and counsel

others about finding a lifemate. And it's rarely presented well by Hollywood and the media, which tend to glorify and mythologize the romantic approach. Thus, it's rarely understood well by those who are eager to find a spouse. The tragedy is that the friendship approach works vastly better than the romantic for many of us, and it's much easier for most of us to navigate. And it's far more likely to produce a strong marriage.

The best news is that it's often more readily available to us. Many, who see no possibility of a romantic relationship with anyone on their horizon, do have a friendship—or the possibility of one—that can grow into a superb marriage relationship. If nothing else, I hope this book opens your mind to the possibility of this happening for you. To that end, let's take a careful look at both of these time-honored paths to marriage.

The Romantic Path
The most storied path to marriage is unquestionably the romantic. It's the one most exalted, far and away, in literature, movies, television, and all forms of media and advertising. It's also the one most people in Western society assume is the normal way we are usually drawn into a serious relationship and end up marrying.

In the popular concept of how two people meet and eventually marry, it's romance that sparks the relationship in the first place. Two strangers meet and, immediately or early on, sense strong chemistry. Within a short time, they're consumed with romantic and sexual desire for each other, at a level neither has experienced in relationships before. Friendship comes after the fact, as they date and grow better acquainted. They not only become best friends, though, but supreme companions who can no longer imagine life as meaningful without the other. They marry, finally, because they're compelled to; their intense longing for each other leaves them no other choice. After being swept into marriage on these romantic winds, they coast on them happily ever after.

In the popular ideal, the true marriage-quality relationship differs starkly from other male-female friendships, even though some may be laden with affection and intimate sharing. It's also on a different plateau from other romantic relationships we may have enjoyed, regardless of the chemistry that drove them. The soul mate relationship is simply *better* in every way. And it brings with it a sense of calling—a conviction that you've found the life companion for whom you were destined before the foundation of time. "You simply know that you know that you know" you've found your match, I heard one pastor put it. "And if you can give a logical reason why you should marry this person, it's not of God."

Of course, most of us realize that the reality falls short of the ideal for many couples we know, who still are very happily married. They got to marriage through a circuitous route, and on the way worked through many doubts about their feelings. And we carry a sinking feeling that we will also need to compromise the ideal at certain points if we're ever to marry at all. Still, we're certain that if we're fortunate enough to get married, it will be romance that propels us there. And we assume this means several things at minimum:

1. The relationship we enjoy with the one we're to marry will be significantly different from relationships of the past. And this person will most likely be someone we haven't met yet, or someone we've put on a pedestal but who so far hasn't been available to us.

2. We will know immediately when we meet, or soon after, that we're romantically attracted to each other, and at a level that recommends marriage. Romance is what will ignite this relationship, while friendship will develop in time.

3. The romantic ecstasy we feel for each other will never wane but, if anything, will strengthen with time.

4. This overwhelming, dizzying bliss will define our marriage throughout the years as we grow old together, and will inject radically greater happiness into our lives.

In the best-case scenario, these expectations may serve us well, if they are the carrot on the stick pulling us into a relationship with the qualities that really *do* work well for marriage. God is good, and he often uses our humanness in this fashion to move us forward. The tragedy comes when these expectations restrict our thinking too greatly and close us off to genuinely good possibilities. We may be too quick to write someone off as not being our type who in reality would be an exceptional match for us. We never give her the chance to prove herself, nor ourself the chance to find how different we would feel if we knew her better.

Many do find wonderful marriages through the romantic path, to be sure. But when a truly happy, healthy, supportive marriage results from a romantically-charged relationship, the process by which it happens differs markedly from the popular stereotype. The white-hot feelings that ignited that relationship always wane and, apart from a short engagement, well before the wedding. But in their place a friendship blossoms that has the best qualities for marriage. The two discover many common interests, shared values, and simple joy in doing the ordinary activities of life together. Most important, they find they deeply *care* for each other, long to see each other prosper, and naturally want to sacrifice for each other. The competitiveness, defensiveness, and selfishness underlying so many romantic relationships just aren't there.

Equally important, they are each mature individuals who together lock into a dream of building a great marriage. Their dream likely carries a sense of mission as well—to grow a loving family, or to serve others in certain ways that they can better do together than singly.

Some romantic affection for each other remains after marrying for sure, and they enjoy being sexually intimate for years. Yet if they're honest, they'll admit that amorous feelings aren't what are driving the relationship anymore, but the higher goal of building a life together and being Best Friends Forever.

Another major difference from the popular stereotype—and the greatest myth buster of all—is that the best romantic relationships often don't begin as such. Many people are surprised to find they're capable of developing strong romantic feelings for someone who was no more than a friend at first. For many of us, appreciating this dynamic and that it can work for us, is the single most important step we can take toward finding our ideal mate.

The Friendship Path

Which brings us to the other way many find their way to a happy marriage.

Nita Tucker writes books and conducts seminars on finding a marriage partner. As a workshop exercise, she asks participants to interview happily married couples about their relationships. One of the questions asked a couple is whether they felt romantically attracted to each other when they first met. Out of more than 1,000 couples interviewed at the time she wrote her first book, more than 80% had responded no, it had taken time for romantic feelings to develop. Yet in time their relationship, which began merely as a friendship with no romantic expectations, blossomed into a deeply fulfilling marriage.[1]

Of course, this is just one survey, and various factors could have skewed the results. Yet more than 1,000 couples were interviewed in good faith. Even if the true percentage is closer to 50% for Americans today, it strongly challenges the popular belief that most blissful marriages begin with a blazing romance. My personal experience, from decades of observing marriages, is that this survey bears up well to reality if we make one adjustment: In perhaps half the cases when friendship develops into marriage, *some* romantic chemistry is present at the start. Yet it's not volcanic and not enough to convince the couple they've found their soul mate. It's just enough to spur some not-too-serious dating or hanging out.

In the other cases, romantic chemistry is absent at first. It does come in time, but not at the monumental level most assume is needed to justify marriage. Yet such a highly supportive friendship develops, with so many benefits to them both, that the couple concludes they'll be far happier married than apart. Indeed, the best-kept secret of good marriages is that moderate romantic and sexual attraction usually makes for a happier marriage than extreme, when it's combined with strong friendship and deep caring for each other.

The friendship path to marriage is actually not one path but many, and great friendships translate into great marriages in a variety of ways.

The long-standing friendship. In one, two longtime friends suddenly and surprisingly discover that it makes great sense to marry. They may never have felt romantic affection for each other before— or perhaps just a little, but not enough to fuel a major dating relationship. Instead, they've been confidants to each other in *other* relationships, and have openly shared together their romantic fantasies for others. They've been famously supportive of each other in countless ways. They've found it instinctive to want each other's best. They've rooted for each other, cheered each other on, and rejoiced when the other succeeded. They've so greatly enjoyed hanging out and sharing intimately, that they may even regard the other as their best friend.

In occasional unguarded moments they've even admitted they wished they loved each other romantically, for their relationship works so well in other ways. But now much time has passed— maybe years; they're older now, wiser, and *different* in many ways. They begin to suspect they could feel romantically attracted and could enjoy physical intimacy—*if* they opened their hearts to it. Commitment to such a relationship just might make the difference.

And so they take a gigantic step of faith, and not without serious fear and trembling, for they clearly recognize the risks ("Why ruin a great friendship by getting married?"). Yet with this step comes unspeakable relief, for the most complex decision of their lives is now resolved, and each takes great comfort in knowing they have chosen not merely a lover, but a wholly faithful friend to be their closest companion for life. Many confirmations begin to come that they're chosen wisely. And the lover part comes too—and often more intensely than they imagined, because of the strong security they feel in this relationship, and the marvelous freedom of knowing they know longer have to prove themselves to anyone.

Their marriage, once consummated, takes on a different flavor from those driven more substantially by romance. Yet, overall, it's a far happier partnership, and one more conducive to building a happy family.

Theirs is the textbook way—you might say the storybook way—that friendship evolves into marriage. Yet it happens much more often than many realize, and not infrequently through a similar odyssey.

In other cases, this same basic story takes some different twists and turns.

Looking up an old friend. In another case, a man who is growing serious about getting married begins to fantasize about what marriage might be like with certain women he has known in the past. A wonderful friend perhaps from childhood, high school, or college, comes to mind—someone he hasn't seen in some time. Perhaps she even hinted at the time that she would be open to a deeper relationship, but he wasn't so inclined then.

Or perhaps he remembers a woman he had dated for a while who proved to be an exemplary friend, yet he broke off the relationship because he felt his romantic feelings weren't strong enough.

Over these years, though, his perspective on marriage has changed. Now he's looking more for kindness and supportiveness in a wife than for beauty and "sharpness"—though he longs for some chemistry, and for someone he can talk to about anything. He begins to wonder if it could work with this companion of the past. He's stunned to find his instincts telling him yes it would. Is he deceiving himself? It is just wishful thinking? He determines to find out.

He looks her up, and is pleased to find that though she has been through a couple of relationships since they last conversed, she's unattached now, and is deeply touched he has contacted her. In the days ahead, as they catch up on many things, he decides simply to level with her and be completely transparent. He admits he has been wondering if—possibly, potentially—they could be happily married. He naturally worries he has blown it all by this confession; maybe she just wants a friend and isn't interested in discussing marriage.

Much to the contrary. She feels like the blood has suddenly been drained out of her, and is at a rare loss for words. When she finally is able to muster a response, she replies that she, too, has wondered just that, and that it makes *a lot* of sense to her. She would be open to dating and staying seriously open to marrying.

The rest is history. Before long they both conclude that their lives are marching on, and they should simply go for it. And they do. Romance comes to them—not on the fiery level of some past and imagined relationships—but substantial enough to bring them great joy and enliven their friendship, which over time proves to be a remarkably solid basis for a wonderful marriage.

Starting from scratch. In many other cases when friendship transforms into marriage, a couple doesn't know each other well when they start dating, but begins a relationship from scratch. Each has their checklist—those features of their ideal mate they've long assumed are non-negotiable. Unfortunately, neither measures up well to the other's list at certain points.

Her body type doesn't match his long-held fantasies very well. And she's from New Jersey, and talks like it; he had dreamed of a woman with a softer, slower, more southern style. And . . . she's a software specialist; is that really a *feminine* vocation? He had imagined being happiest with a school teacher or nurse, that is, with someone following a more traditional female career.

Speaking of body type, *he's* two inches shorter than her; she had long dreamed her prince would tower over her. And he's a musician, not the former high school football all-star she had dreamed of courting her. *And* he's a band teacher in a public school. A stable profession, yes, and productive, unquestionably. But not at a salary likely to support her at the lifestyle to which she has become accustomed of fantasizing.

But she discovers he's an exceptional listener. He listens patiently and seems genuinely interested as she details challenges at work. He empathizes with her frustrations but isn't trigger-happy to offer solutions. And he remembers! Details from her childhood and past, the names of friends and family members, and data about them she takes pains to describe—minutia important to her but often difficult for past boyfriends to absorb.

He's also there when she falls sick and is unable to work for two weeks. He stops by each morning on the way to school, brings her breakfast and walks her dog. He returns in the evening and fixes dinner for her. He escorts her to the doctor several times, and keeps her supplied with videos to watch while bed-ridden. His compassion for her is authentic, and she senses it.

Though she has never dated a musician before, she finds his passion for music and performing engaging. His love for students and for helping them sharpen their craft deeply touches her. As does the affection students and parents have for him, and she delights in attending his school concerts. She also enjoys tagging along with him to gigs at local restaurants, where he performs a solo keyboard stint. His ability to perform confidently in front of audiences both large and small greatly impresses her.

They also discover many points of common interest: a mutual love for skiing, bowling, watching vintage movies, and for helping together on Sunday afternoons at a local shelter.

Within a short time, they're walking in such a natural lockstep that each thinks of the other as their best friend. Romantic affection comes naturally to them. While not as explosive as in certain past relationships, it's not nearly so anxiety-ridden either. Neither is possessed with that horrid neediness that drives so many romantic relationships, where one worries constantly about how responsive their partner will be on their next date. Neither worries at all about the other using sex manipulatively.

In the months these two have dated, a relationship has evolved that's more friendship based than romantic. Yet make no mistake about it. These two *love* each other, and in the most deep, vibrant way needed for the best possible marriage. It takes a while for each to shed their expectations of the perfect mate, and to adapt to the startling reality that they've found their ideal in each other. They do make this adjustment, though, and with it comes the clear conclusion they should marry.

Many go through a "paradigm shift" similar to this couple's in their own journey to marriage. It happens to many who are active daters and veterans of many failed romantic relationships, who in time discover that certain expectations and ideals have been working against finding the right partner. God graciously nudges them to this point, by bringing into their life an exceptional friend who's a far better match for them than any of their past romantic companions. And they're wise and humble enough to let him open their eyes to what they've found.

Using friendship as a strategy in an ongoing relationship. In the cases we've looked at so far of marriage springing from friendship, two people have worked through certain issues, revised expectations, and reached certain conclusions more or less simultaneously. Life is often not so simple, though. Many good relationships follow a more complex path where, for a while, one feels more in love and more committed to the hope of marriage than the other. This, of course, is often true in romantically-charged relationships, where one is clearly the pursuer and the other the pursued. Yet even in friendships with marriage potential, one may see that possibility and long for it more quickly than the other.

If you're in a relationship where your hope for something more runs stronger than your partner's, you need first to decide if it's worth the effort to try to win this person over. If your longing is based on a need for conquest or to prove yourself, or on an obsessive romantic or sexual need, you do best to abandon your hope and to look for a relationship where your needs and motives are different. But if you truly care for her, and genuinely believe she'll be better off in a lifetime relationship with you—and if you believe you're more naturally capable of seeing around the bend and grasping this vision than she is—then the effort to win her hand may be worthwhile.

We're schooled in western society to think that winning someone's hand in marriage depends on our ability to be romantic, seductive, sharp-witted, intellectually keen, successful, impressively skilled. Yet if God has drawn you into a relationship with someone for the purpose of marrying, you'll most likely win him over simply by being his best possible friend. Some effort to present yourself well and appeal to him romantically is important, as a compassionate move toward him and an acquiescence to his humanness. But being her friend is more likely to take you the distance—and for most of us, it's a far more achievable goal than striving to impress her romantically, or with what a fine specimen of humanity we are.

And so, yes, I'm suggesting that friendship can be a *strategy* for turning someone's heart more fully toward you and toward the idea of marrying you.

You may naturally object (and I hope you do initially) that it's wrong even to broach the idea of using friendship as a "strategy" in relationships. If it's God's intention that you marry someone, won't this come about naturally, without heroic effort on your part? And doesn't the notion of friendship as a strategy make a mockery of friendship itself? Isn't friendship about acting sacrificially, and loving someone without hope of personal benefit? To speak of friendship as a strategy seems to be saying we should use it selfishly, to manipulate another for our own purpose.

Many do use the show of friendship in ways that are manipulative and sadly inappropriate. The man who sends a woman flowers and does her favors solely from the hope of scoring sexually is treating her unkindly, by attempting to appear as her friend purely for his selfish advantage.

But if you're in a relationship with someone whom you love good-heartedly, and you truly desire God's best for this person, then the dynamics are different. For one thing, God may use you as an agent of change with this person. Your friend may not automatically recognize your potential as a marriage partner, nor how stunningly his life would be enriched by marrying you. He's a product of his past, and carries his own biases and misplaced expectations. He's viewing you through these filters, and that tendency simply goes with his being human—no matter how open-minded he may be. God won't necessarily visit him in the night with a dramatic revelation, telling him he should view you and his future differently. God may expect you to provide him a *demonstration* of why he should.

Also, as noble as it may be to think we shouldn't want any benefit from being someone's friend, this notion misses friendship's essence. In a healthy friendship, you naturally want and will the best for the other, unquestionably. But you also greatly enjoy this person's company. Without this second dynamic, there's no *friendship* but just a sacrificial relationship. Friendship is for "people who need people," and without this mutual hope for enjoyment of the friendship, it can never thrive.

I submit to you also that it's psychologically impossible to do an act of kindness to a friend and not to want certain benefits in return. We're simply wired as humans to want this reciprocity. And it's part of what generates the dynamic chemistry of friendship: we want to see our friend benefit, but us also—*and* the friendship itself, which has a life of its own and provides us with an important identity that benefits us both.

It is, then, fully legitimate to do those things we believe will improve a friendship, deepen it, and make it more what God intends. I wish there were a better word than "strategy" to describe this effort, for, yes, the term sounds clinical and possibly manipulative. But the process I'm speaking of is a gracious and compassionate one in the highest sense, and one that God inspires.

Jack and Priscilla met through an Internet dating service, and hit it off well communicating online. They shared some strong common interests, had a similar spiritual background, and found each other friendly and caring. When they finally met in person, though, Jack was disappointed by Priscilla's appearance. She was attractive in her own way, he realized, and other men might find her so. But she wasn't attractive in *his* way. She weighed a bit more than her online photos indicated, and lacked certain features of the women of Jack's fantasies.

Priscilla also recognized that Jack wasn't George Clooney, but she didn't care. She was drawn to his big-heartedness, and quickly knew she wanted to marry him. Jack wasn't as sure; he liked Priscilla enormously as a friend, but worried that the physical issue might keep him from falling in love with her. He was a deep enough thinker, though, to realize his outlook might be skewed, and he decided at least to date Priscilla for a while and "give it some time."

On the third date, rightly or wrongly, Jack decided to level with Priscilla. He told her she was extraordinary and the answer to his dreams in many ways. Yet she didn't fit certain fantasies about his ideal mate's appearance, which he had long held and didn't know how to discard. This wasn't her problem, he stressed repeatedly, but his own hang-up. Still, he was who he was and didn't know how to get beyond this hurdle; perhaps it was God's way of showing that he didn't wish them to marry?

Priscilla understandably was hurt. Yet she was farsighted enough to sense a bigger picture. She realized Jack was a product of his past, and she felt instinctively that with time, he would see her differently. She told him she wanted to continue dating anyway, and for the moment was willing to be patient. Jack was relieved. Priscilla was already proving to be such an exceptional friend that he didn't want to let her go.

Priscilla determined to be Jack's best conceivable friend, and to let him experience firsthand some benefits he would enjoy if he married her. Her daily commute brought her near his home, and her workday started earlier than his. So she began making his lunch and dropping it by on her way to work. This saved Jack a daily task he disliked, and Priscilla's food choices were far more creative and tasty than his. She also wove him a beautiful tweed jacket and gave it to him on his October birthday.

Then, after smoke from a chimney fire damaged several rooms in Jack's home, she spent a long weekend helping him clean up.

I must stress that Priscilla did these things because she *wanted* to. Since such acts of kindness were natural to her, they were a perfect way to demonstrate to Jack the sort of friend she would be to him in marriage. You shouldn't force yourself to be someone you're not, or wouldn't be once married, in order to win your partner over. But if you instinctively enjoy being helpful in certain ways, it can make sense to treat your partner generously to such behavior—if the relationship is ripe for it.

It made all the difference in Priscilla's case. Her patient supportiveness not only deeply moved Jack, but his family and friends as well. One day his pastor remarked to him, "Jack, you could look till you're 100 and never find a better match." Jack knew his pastor was right. He took the next day off from work, in order to pray about what to do. As he reflected on his past several months with Priscilla, he realized that his reservations about her appearance were no longer nearly as important. What he had in her was a supreme companion, a best friend for life. No other woman's beauty, sexiness or charm could compare to Priscilla's *heart*—and he knew *that* was what he wanted to marry. He resolved to propose to her that evening.

Seeing New Possibilities

I've seen countless examples like Priscilla and Jack's, where one person's patient demonstration of friendship so touched the heart of their less-convinced partner, that it changed the course of the relationship. The truth is that each of us has a similar capacity to transform a relationship, simply by being the best sort of friend. In the pages ahead, I'll look closely at what this friendship strategy can mean in your own case, and how it can greatly improve your prospects for finding someone wonderful to marry.

To be sure, what makes for effective friendship strategy varies greatly from person to person. It has much more to do with an attitude—a mindset—than with specific behavior. Indeed, you may end up doing many of the same things you would to build a more romantically-charged relationship.

But your *premise* is different, and that can make a considerable difference in your confidence, in finding the right person, and in successfully seeing the relationship through to marriage. You are striving to be a *friend* to your companion—and even if you aren't the most romantic or seductive person ever to walk this planet, you do have the ability to touch this person's heart in a way that may resonate much more deeply. I say "may," for it depends on finding the right person, who is flexible and big-hearted enough to recognize they may need to grow in their thinking about love and marriage. They need to be humble enough to accept that their checklist for the perfect mate may need some revising, and that God's best for them may differ from their fantasies.

Yet the world is chock full of such people, and they make vastly better marriage partners than those who are stuck on finding someone who perfectly meets their romantic ideals. And for each of us, a multitude of such people is out there who will be open to marrying us, if we make the effort to be a special friend to them.

Whether you're looking for a special friend to marry, or are in a relationship where you're trying to be such a friend, this path is far more likely to lead you to a happy and successful marriage than the romantic approach. *Liberating. Life-giving.* These are the terms that best describe it. In the next chapter, we'll look more carefully at why the friendship path to marriage trumps the romantic in every way.

Three

* * * * * * * * * *

The Remarkable Benefits of the Friendship Path

OKAY, LET'S BE REALISTIC.

None of us moves from singleness to marriage by a straight path that we can fully envision in advance. We are always like a man who sets out to travel a region that hasn't been fully charted. Like him, we have a map that's partly accurate, which is important, for it gets us moving. But we constantly find ourselves in uncharted territory and are surprised at every turn. Sometimes we're surprised by rejection and disappointment. But if we persevere and hang in there long enough, we're often surprised by a joyous victory.

It's also impossible to know just how much romantic intensity will be there for us in the relationship that finally leads to marriage, or in the marriage itself. It varies considerably from couple to couple, and from partner to partner within couples. It's not unusual for one partner to feel stronger romantic attraction or sexual desire, while the other is drawn to the relationship more for companionship. There are many models that work for couples in good marriages, and many that will work for you also. It's important to keep an open mind about this as you look for someone to marry.

Still, certain givens are always there in the journey to marriage. *One is that you marry a human being, not a fantasy.* Nothing is more important to keep in mind as you look for a spouse. The problem is that fantasy is always more enticing than reality. Always. Always. Always. Yet no one enters a happy marriage without shedding their fantasies at certain points. There's always at least some negotiation of ideals and expectations you've long held dear, and in many cases considerable "revising of the map."

To be sure, it's *important* to have your checklist—a clear idea of the qualities you most want in the one you marry—for it helps you eliminate certain prospects who definitely wouldn't be good companions for you. Your checklist also inspires you to get moving, and to "test the waters" with certain people who seem to match your ideals. But once in a relationship, you need to throw out that checklist. It's based so greatly on cultural factors, hormones, the experiences of others who are different than you, and a woefully limited understanding of what will make you happiest as the years unfold, that you should give it minimal weight once you're in a relationship that, for whatever reasons, seems to be working well. Instead, you should let this person prove herself on her own merits.

Even more important, you should humbly consider whether God in his providence is showing you, through the weight of evidence in this relationship, that he has given you someone who will make a splendid life companion for you. Consider that God knows what will most contribute to your future happiness infinitely better than you do. In addition, he is as concerned with how your relationship with your spouse will help you grow and mature as he is with your fulfillment in marriage. God doesn't want you to marry someone with whom you're miserable or not attracted sexually, nor someone who treats you poorly—don't worry. But the partner he provides for you *will* break your fantasies at certain points—that much is guaranteed.

No matter how perfectly matched you are with the person you choose to marry, your feelings for this person will undergo some change as the relationship develops. If you're driven by intense romantic longing for her at first, that intensity will diminish over time. This is because romantic love at the moonstruck level springs in part from the relationship's newness, the initial sense of mystery, and your intrigue with your partner—all of which ebb as you grow more familiar with this individual.

When the relationship is more friendship driven at first, on the other hand, romantic attraction can actually grow over time. This growth in romantic love can result from discovering qualities in your partner, and potential in the relationship, that you hadn't appreciated before. It can also spring from the security you enjoy with this person, and the permission you feel to be fully human. It can also come, I'm convinced, as a gracious gift of God—a reward for the care and compassion you've shown toward him or her.

Your feelings for this person will fluctuate, though. You'll feel greater romantic attraction on certain days and during certain periods than others. Mood swings are *normal* in love relationships, even for those of us who consider ourselves stable emotionally.

For the vast majority of us, a happy marriage will come more than we currently imagine from a relationship based on friendship more than romance. We may get to that point by different ways. We may start by falling head over heels in love with someone who seems to match our romantic fantasies in every way. But with time comes many reality checks, and our fantasies are punctured one by one. In the past, we would have run away as the romantic flame began to whimper. But this time a beautiful, supportive friendship grows, which draws us in for its own reasons, and provides a superb basis for a strong marriage.

Or the relationship may be more friendship based from the start. Shedding our fantasies in this case involves adjusting our outlook on what constitutes marriage-quality love and the basis for a happy marriage.

Or we may take a path somewhere between these extremes. Regardless how we get there, the happy marriage for us is going to spring more from friendship than romance. To be sure, many do end up in marriages that are more romantically charged than friendship driven. They marry before their romantic feelings have a chance to simmer, and may barely know the person with whom they're joining hands for life. Even if we assume a best-case scenario for such couples—that romantic feelings stay intense till death do them part (a rare occurrence)—the marriage that's based more solidly on friendship is *still* the happier one. There are at least five reasons this is so.

• **Less pressure.** The most intense romantic relationships are always, by their very nature, high maintenance. It's the high-maintenance part that fuels romantic and sexual desire in the first place. You sense your partner is too good for you, and fear she'll lose interest and abandon you. The challenge you face in winning her affection, and the high risk involved, gives way to "the thrill of the chase," and the smallest successes and the faintest hopes are intoxicating to you. You live for the moments when your partner is responsive, and this obsessive longing—identical to the pull of drug or alcohol addiction—is what you perceive as romantic love.

At the same time, you feel under constant pressure to *be* good enough for your partner. *Striving* is the word for it; you're never free from the sinking feeling that there's something more you need to do to win and retain his affection. And the more intense your romantic yearning, the more greatly you fear that someone else may catch his eye and do a better job pleasing him than you can. Despite his reassurances, you never shake the sense that you're in competition for his love.

When the marriage is more friendship based, on the other hand, this pressure to perform and compete is swept away. You long to be a supportive partner to your spouse, and so you do carry a certain burden, for sure. But it springs from a heart of compassion for her, and from wanting her best; that horrid sense that the relationship *depends* on how supportive and impressive you are just isn't there. And of course it's reciprocal; you live in a spirit of mutual support; your spouse is far more than a romantic partner—she's your best friend on this earth, and a *help*mate to you in the truest sense.

• **The sexual relationship.** There's no point where we're more prone to overrate the potential of a romantically-charged marriage, and underrate the prospects of a more friendship-based one, than this. It's the hope of a dizzying, ecstatic sexual experience that, more than anything else, draws us into the romantic relationship. It's extraordinarily difficult to keep our head at such a time and to think logically about where the relationship will head. Yet the stark reality is that most who marry primarily for romance and sex are bitterly disappointed within a short time.

The monumental level of sexual desire initially there in the marriage begins to dwindle, as the novelty of being physically intimate wears off and familiarity sets in. So often, too, when romance and sex are the major force driving two people to marry, they've neglected other areas of their relationship and simply don't know each other well. As they begin to discover each other's human side, the fantasy image of the perfect mate they thought they had married— that had fueled their intense desire—shatters. Typically, they haven't developed good communication skills. The many stresses that result from the challenge of living together have a cooling effect on sexual desire.

Those who marry more from friendship, on the other hand, are much better positioned to enjoy long-term sexual happiness. Because they haven't built up such extravagant expectations, they are free to be surprised, and often are. Simply, the brain is our most potent sexual organ, and we each are far more able to *choose* to enjoy sex with a given person than we normally realize. Not with every person, to be sure, but to a major degree with the person we marry—God has built this capacity into us. And we may enter the sexual relationship with our spouse strongly confident that God is intent on blessing it and giving us joy in being physically intimate, providing, that is, other factors in the marriage are right.

These factors are more likely to *be* right in the friendship-driven marriage. You likely enjoy good communication and strong support. From that foundation, a joyful sexual relationship can blossom. Because you're confident with your partner and under no pressure to impress, you feel free to be sexual—to be human, playful, experimental—and to talk freely about your hopes and fears related to sex. You enjoy the freedom to fail and try again that's so critical to the success of any sexual relationship. And because you have less invested in the sexual relationship than those in romantically-based marriages, you are more naturally patient with your partner, and able to give yourself unselfishly. The result, of course, is reciprocal: your partner responds compassionately to you, and the supportive spirit that results increases the joy of sex for you both.

Give a marriage five, ten, twenty years, or many more, and those who've married from friendship are likely to tell you that the joy of being physically intimate has increased over this time, as they've grown to know each other better and learned how to respond best to each other's needs—and as they've come to understand themselves better as well. Those who married *for* sex and romance, on the other hand—if their marriage has survived—will more likely talk of disappointment and declining pleasure in their physical relationship.

• **Much more to hold your interest.** Whatever benefits a friendship-based marriage may confer on physical intimacy, there's a broader reason why this marriage is usually the happier one. It's the simple fact that you enjoy doing so many things together. No matter how thrilling love making may be, the constraint of other responsibilities—and the sheer limits of your endurance (!)—mean that only a small portion of the marriage is ever devoted to sex. You may enjoy other romantic activities, to be sure—the candlelight dinner, the dance, the occasional cruise. Yet unavoidably, the vast majority of your waking moments in any marriage are spent doing things not so obviously intoxicating.

The multitude of tasks involved in managing a home takes substantial time. And with children comes vast attention devoted to raising a family. Those who marry primarily for romance and sex often find domestic responsibilities a nuisance—a necessary evil to endure for the real prize of winning time to be physically intimate. They often resent the demands of parenting as well. They may strive to be good parents. Yet their hearts aren't fully in it. They long for the greater freedom and simplicity their life together enjoyed before parenting stole so much of it away. And they yearn for the romantic euphoria of those early days, when they enjoyed generous private time, and their only focus was on keeping each other happy.

Those who marry for friendship, on the other hand, are much more likely to enjoy domestic tasks, and even to delight greatly in all the challenges of building a home and raising a family. Because at the heart of their friendship is joy in doing creative things together, building a *life* together is a monumental adventure and a deeply meaningful goal. And because friendship is what unites them in marriage, they instinctively love sharing it with their children—the new flesh-and-blood companions God brings into their life. Parenting is a natural fit for them.

And when it comes to fun and leisure activities, friends are likely to have more things they enjoy doing together than romantic partners. In the friendship-based marriage, recreational activities are ends in themselves, and not just a way to pass the time between intimate encounters. The chance to see a movie, go bowling, visit a museum, or take in a concert—these are major luxuries to such couples who enjoy such pastimes. Activities like these bring continual spice and celebration to a married life already filled with such meaning.

Friends who are joined in marriage are also much more likely to take on missions together. The heart of compassion they have for each other naturally extends to others in need. Many such couples find ways to mutually serve others that fit wonderfully well with their gifts and lifestyle. They may host a Bible study, open their home to a youth ministry, or volunteer together at a shelter or nursing home—to note some of the more conventional options. I've known many couples who not only help others tremendously through such shared service but also find great joy and fulfillment in it. For some couples, a mutual mission becomes nothing less than the cornerstone of their marriage.

• **You maintain your identity.** A friend confessed to me that he once had the opportunity to marry a woman whom he worshiped. "I thank God it never happened," he explained, "for then I would have ceased to be who I am."

My friend's transparent comment brings us to another aspect of marital happiness that we seldom think about much in advance, but that's critical to our day-to-day contentment once married. The more greatly you are dazed with romantic love for your partner, the more likely it is that the dreams and aspirations you held dear prior to the relationship—those things most uniquely you—get put on the back burner. You're now consumed with the relationship, with keeping it stable and your partner happy. Of course, you devote yourself convinced that here lies your greatest happiness, and that no sacrifice of otherwise worthy goals is too great to enjoy the relationship's benefits. Yet the sacrifice of your individuality *is* too great, for with it goes the source of an even higher level of happiness, which never forces itself on you, but is central to how God has made you as an individual. Over time, you find immense joy in using the distinctive gifts God has given you, and in pursuing the dreams he places in your heart. A relationship that supports your dreams, and helps you find the heart and courage to follow them, is life-giving in the most profound sense. A relationship that discourages you from being who you are chokes the breath of life within you.

Like the drug addict willing to sell his soul to enjoy brief euphoria, those overcome with romantic love too often are willing to let go of their identity to enjoy the relationship's occasional ecstasy.

A different spirit prevails in the marriage based more on friendship. Your romantic attraction isn't at such an addictive level. You're free enough from preoccupation with it still to be yourself; marriage doesn't substantially change your personality or annul your creative drives. The hopes and dreams generic to your temperament have room to grow and thrive. And in the supportive climate of this marriage, they do thrive. Your spouse encourages you to pursue the desires of your heart, cheers you on, rejoices with you in your victories and comforts you in your setbacks. Your individuality not only remains intact but is nurtured in the best possible ways.

Joy is the natural byproduct of realizing your potential, and a major reason the friendship marriage trumps the romantic in happiness.

• **Your relationship with God.** How often we hear it said, "Don't marry someone whom you can possibly live without." It's probably the most common advice offered when one supposedly wiser friend counsels a less-wise friend on finding a spouse. It's also the mantra of many Christian talks and books on mate seeking. And on the surface it sounds so right. Why would you possibly want to marry someone without whom you would still be happy? Shouldn't you hold out for that one person who captures your heart so totally that life would be meaningless without her?

Yet consider for a moment what that *really* would be like. You would be horribly needy in such a relationship. Your happiness would depend hugely on how your partner treats you. You would have little life of your own anymore. Your love for this person would be obsessive. And the scary bottom line: this person would be your god.

This is precisely the case in so many romantic relationships. In the fiery-hot romance, your partner is the center of your universe, drawing your strongest affection and highest devotion. Your greatest concern is with keeping him happy and responsive, and no sacrifice seems too great. You have little mental energy left for a relationship with God, nor likely much concern for it, apart from looking to him to bless the relationship. Not to mention that a relationship with God is about seeking his guidance and following it, but your spouse has your primary allegiance.

We do well here to remember the frequent biblical admonitions against idolatry. Idolatry in Scripture, most literally, is about misplaced worship. The idolaters so resoundingly condemned in the Old Testament actually bowed down to wooden carvings, and looked to these inanimate creations for godlike protection and help. We come dangerously close to this, though, when anything is more important to us than God, and commands our highest devotion and affection. We're not only on dangerous ground spiritually then, but emotionally, for we're failing to live as God intends, and thus depriving ourselves of significant happiness. God has created us to find our greatest joy in a relationship with him, where we seek to put him first in everything.

This is another reason—and a major one—why moderate romantic attraction works best in marriage, especially when strong friendship is central. You take great joy in your spouse. Yet because you still have a life of your own, you have room for a relationship with God, and the potential to make him Lord of your life. God then is able to "get your ear"—to enlighten you about your gifts and his special plans for you, and to give you the courage for steps of faith. This guidance factor is so vital to experiencing purpose and living productively. The friendship-based marriage provides the climate in which this relationship with God can thrive, and the benefits that follow are insurmountable.

• **The cooperative factor.** More generally, this sort of marriage also best enables and inspires a couple to work together in all the ways necessary to make the marriage happy. Here's what I mean: We imagine that marriage is an estate that confers happiness or misery on us without our permission, and that we're helpless to do much about it once the ship sets sail. Happiness comes if we're fortunate enough to choose the perfect mate who matches all our ideals, and we then experience no setbacks once married that diminish our joy. Marital bliss depends upon our spouse, "the relationship," and a host of unforeseen circumstances over which we have little control.

This belief that we're passive victims when it comes to happiness in marriage leads many to an obsessive search for just the right mate. Then, once they think they've found her or him, they wait endlessly to marry, never confident that marriage will bestow enough happiness to make the plunge worth taking.

In truth, our happiness in marriage depends vastly more on factors we can control than on those we can't. This is true on the individual, psychological level to a stunning extent. My simple decision to choose to be happy in the day-to-day reality of marriage has more to do with the joy I experience than with how my spouse treats me or with any unpredictable circumstances.

Yet watch out when two people embrace this concept *together.* When a couple consciously decides to dedicate themselves for a lifetime to each other's happiness, and to their children's, and to making the marriage a blessing to all whose lives they touch, the effect is powerful beyond any human words.

Two romantic partners may find it easy to say they'll devote their lives to making each other happy. Carrying it out is difficult, though, if romantic attraction is primarily what has drawn them together, for each is driven more by self-interest than their partner's. Yet the potential for two friends with great compassion for each other to dedicate themselves to each other's happiness in marriage, and then carry out that intent on many levels, is enormous. Happiness for these two is not a matter of fate, not something "in the cards." They hold the key to creating it; and, when two caring friends marry, invariably they do exactly that. Two people who at one point may have assumed that romance held the key to marital bliss are "surprised by joy," to use C. S. Lewis's term. They're astonished to find that their choice to marry more for friendship has positioned them to carve out a deeply fulfilling married life, and one that's the envy of others.

I call this ability of a fortunate couple to commit to each other's happiness in marriage "the cooperative factor." Romantic partners find it difficult to embrace this commitment, in spite of lip service to it, because of their desire to keep the enjoyment of physical intimacy so supremely central. It's the opposite for those who marry more from friendship. Because they are not so addicted to the romantic part, they are freer to focus on the many other areas that make or break the marriage. And they are better able simply to will to make these areas good, because they more instinctively care about each other's happiness.

Indeed, the cooperative factor is more at the heart of why some marriages are happy and others aren't, than anything else. It is one thing, and a blessed discovery, to stumble on this key to happiness once married. But appreciating it in advance can help you over the hump if you're wrestling with whether to turn a relationship into marriage that is all heart but less electrifying romantically than you had hoped. It's also an extremely helpful principle to keep in mind if you're looking for someone to marry. Understanding it will finetune your instincts to avoid those relationships that won't work well for you, and more readily recognize those that, even surprisingly, will.

• **Friendships outside the marriage.** The assumption that marriage bestows much of its happiness or misery on us apart from our own effort is tragic, for it blinds us to seeing that marriage is what *we* make of it—and that two caring partners have the capacity to carve out a truly happy life together. An equally tragic assumption is that our relationship with our spouse is a *panacea* as far as happiness is concerned. We imagine that in the right marriage, our spouse meets all of our social, emotional, intellectual, and spiritual needs— and meets them far better than any other earthly companion ever has or possibly can. Marriage is thus a quantum leap forward for us socially, we suppose, and a huge jump from mediocrity to bliss.

Yet no companion, no matter how wonderful, possesses this

godlike ability to be all things to us.

It's easy to miss this point, since we do have an obvious need that our spouse alone is to meet. God has so designed marriage that, till death do us part, our spouse is to be our only lover. We're to look to this person alone to meet our romantic and sexual needs. We are far happier staying faithful, and any fantasy that we might be happier seeking physical intimacy outside the marriage will only lead to heartache for us and heartbreak for our partner. If you understand and respect this point, then it may seem natural to assume that your spouse should provide all of your other companionship needs as well, and be the one best able to do so.

Yet as we move beyond romantic intimacy, the dynamics begin to change. Yes, our spouse is our most *important* earthly friend. Yet God never intends him or her to be our *only* friend, nor necessarily the one who best meets certain needs. We continue to need the support of other friends and the intellectual and creative stimulation that certain people bring us, who may be the ones who can best help us grow in particular areas.

I think of one marriage in which the wife is a concert cellist. Her husband plays guitar but not at a professional level, and he doesn't aspire to perform. While highly supportive of her career goals, he has little understanding of classical music. She thus needs much artistic stimulation from friends and professionals outside the marriage, a reality with which her husband fortunately is quite comfortable.

Their example may be more extreme than most, but not unreasonably so. No matter how well-matched any two married people are, each still has unique interests, tastes, preferences, and professional aspirations. Each needs others who can support them and encourage their growth at these points. While their friendship with their spouse must stay central through everything, it cannot be expected to meet every need.

Those in heavily romantic relationships often feel so possessive of their spouse's heart and time that they're intimidated by this person's other friendships. They're instinctively jealous of their mate's opposite-sex friends especially, and of any friendship that draws significant time away from the marriage. Those in friendship-based marriages, though, see life through a different filter. They're grateful for each other's bigger circle of friends, for it enriches their own life too, and takes the pressure off them to have to be all things to their spouse. The wonderful freedom to nurture and enjoy friendships outside the marriage is another reason, and a major one, why this marriage is typically happier.

• **Confidence about the future.** There's at least one more significant reason why the friendship-based marriage is happier than the romantic, and it has to do with our psychology. We are creatures of hope as humans, and the hope we experience at any given moment has much to do with the happiness we feel then. As Daniel Gilbert notes in *Stumbling on Happiness,* our capacity to imagine the future is the mental function that most clearly differentiates us from all other animals.[2] And envision the future we do. We who are analytical dwell on the future so greatly that we find it impossible to enjoy the moment more than briefly if we're not strongly confident life will still be as good for us, or better, in the days, months, and years ahead.

The pleasures of a romantic relationship may be intense at times. But it's impossible to enjoy them without also imagining what the future holds. The thinking person sees all around him marriages that began on the mountaintop of ecstasy but ended in the valley of recrimination and divorce. He knows his own marriage is based strongly on his and his partner's self-interest, which either might someday find better satisfied in a different relationship. It's hard not to fear their relationship may eventually face challenges it can't survive. That sinking feeling—that projection—is part of the emotion he experiences even at the marriage's best moments, and strongly affects his happiness.

When the marriage is based on a vibrant friendship, on the other hand, you're not riddled with anxiety that your spouse may walk out on you at some point. You're confident she'll stay faithful. Even more important, you're able to embrace hope. As you come to appreciate the benefits of a friendship-based marriage, you naturally enjoy hope that it will be better in certain ways in the future, as you grow a family and create an evolving life together, building as you go on the numerous advantages this marriage bestows.

Indeed, it may well be said that hope is the friendship marriage's greatest gift to you, for it contributes substantially to the happiness you experience at any given time.

The Road Less Traveled
In the book I just mentioned, *Stumbling on Happiness*, Daniel Gilbert stresses that we humans are poor judges of our own future happiness. We make many choices that we sincerely believe will improve our life and lead to greater joy. We even spend considerable time deliberating them. Then we're surprised to find that the happiness we expected doesn't transpire. This is because we base our assumptions about the future upon our present feelings. We miss that we'll be *a different person* in the future. Life will change us in certain ways, and what makes us happy then will be different from what does now.

We're thus likely to need some paradigm shifts, even major ones, if we're to chart our future successfully. There's no area where this is truer than our outlook on marriage. We base our vision of future marital bliss upon our past dating experiences and fantasies that have long tantalized us. We imagine a happy marriage to be one long continuation of the romantic ecstasy we enjoyed in a favorite dating relationship or hoped-for one. We fail to consider how marriage will change us, and how our needs will be different as married life unfolds.

Romance will continue to be important, but not close to our greatest concern. Far more important to our day-to-day contentment will be the level of friendship we enjoy with our spouse, that person's care for us, and the simple joy we experience in the many activities of building our life together. Friendship makes or breaks a marriage, and contributes vastly more to our happiness than anything else.

All of this is welcome news if you're considering marrying someone who in a heartbeat you would term your best friend, yet who falls short of your romantic fantasies in certain ways. But it's equally reassuring if you're unattached and wondering if you can possibly muster the heart to begin looking again. Finding a special friend to marry is a less intimidating goal for most of us than searching for the perfect romantic companion. What you'll have to do to win this person's heart seems more achievable—and is. You can be a caring friend to someone who would be an exceptional life companion for you, and do it so effectively that this person will want to marry you. Suddenly the dream of finding the right partner seems within reach!

And suddenly the pool of potential candidates seems much larger. Perhaps you quickly realize that a certain longtime friend whom you've overlooked as a marriage possibility in fact would make a splendid life partner for you. Or a more recent acquaintance whom you've too quickly discounted as not your type is, in fact, worth getting to know, and deserves a chance to prove herself. If such prospects don't seem to be on the immediate horizon, I hope you're more confident now that they may not be too distant, and that finding someone right for you is no longer the impossible dream. And I'll do my best in the pages ahead to give you the direction you need to find and reap a golden opportunity.

First, though, I want to look carefully at some attitudes that strongly affect our success or failure in finding someone to marry. These include our desire for marriage, our optimism about finding someone, our alertness to opportunities, and our willingness to make certain personal changes. When our attitude isn't what it should be at any of these points, we can get stuck in our search for marriage, and are likely to sabotage good opportunities. Reshaping these attitudes where necessary can make every difference in achieving our

dream. So in the next section, we'll turn our attention to these matters of heart and outlook that are so vital to our quest for marriage.

(If you're confident your attitude is good at these different points,
feel free of course to jump ahead to the practical material in part
three. But if you're puzzled why good opportunities often go bad
for you, or just need encouragement to stay in the race, then please
take the time to read this next section carefully. It's often surprising
how simple changes in attitude and thinking can radically improve
our success in relationships.)

Part Two

* * * * * * * * * *

Setting Your Heart
Toward
Getting Married

Four

* * * * * * * * * *

A God-Given Desire

SIMPLY RESOLVING THAT YOU WANT TO FIND A FRIEND to marry is a huge step forward in your search for a spouse. Understanding that friendship in marriage is more important even than romance clears your field of vision, opening your eyes to new possibilities, and increasing your field of potential prospects, sometimes remarkably.

Equally important is resolving that you really *want* to get married. This is another point where the journey to marriage frequently stalls for well-intentioned souls, who often don't recognize how greatly insufficient desire is holding them back from finding someone. Before going further, I want to look closely at the importance of motivation in seeking a mate, and encourage you to consider seriously whether your own desire to marry is adequate to move you forward.

We naturally recognize the critical role of desire in most areas of accomplishment. Indeed, how often we hear it said! The tennis player who most wanted to win the championship did. Or the candidate who most wanted the governorship won the election. Or, following a devastating accident and against every odd, a woman regained her ability to walk, because her will to gain it back was so strong.

We nod our heads and readily agree. The most challenging goals are achieved by those with the greatest passion to reach them. That's obvious to us, a no-brainer.

And it's just as true with us. When we look carefully at our own life, we find we've made our greatest strides in education, career, and so many areas, when we've done what we most loved doing, and pursued goals we most dearly wanted to achieve. Deep motivation is always the driving force behind our most important accomplishments and victories.

But what about getting married? How important is *motivation* to finding a partner, building a relationship, walking the aisle, and launching a successful marriage? Is a strong desire to marry likely to help or hinder us? This is a question we rarely hear addressed in any meaningful way at all. Yet I want to begin this chapter with two possibly radical thoughts: One is that the reason many people who believe they want to get married don't, is because their desire to marry isn't strong enough. The other is that your desire for marriage, even though it might seem substantial, may not be as strong as it needs to be.

Let me hasten to say that I'm speaking of the desire not just for a wonderful relationship, but *for marriage itself* and all the benefits it provides. Just how strong is *that* longing within you?

Not strong enough for many singles today, Susan Page argues in her excellent book, *If I'm So Wonderful, Why Am I Still Single?*[3] Ambivalence keeps more singles from marrying today than any other factor, Page argues. So many who claim they want to be married, and are more than ready, aren't really certain they want to sacrifice the benefits of singleness for a permanent relationship. Social changes over the past several decades have fostered what Page terms an "age of ambivalence" among modern singles.[4] It's vastly more acceptable now than a generation ago to delay marriage or never marry. And a singles culture has exploded that, though its social groups, programs, publications, and Internet presence, promotes the benefits of the unmarried life and urges singles to make the most of it. Page comments:

> In recent decades, singles have banded together to stand up to the larger society that views singles as flawed human beings. This "singles movement" has, fortunately, largely succeeded in achieving general acceptance of the single lifestyle. But it has also created an attractive alternative to coupling up, leaving a generation caught between two appealing choices.[5]

This sea change in how society views singleness has benefited singles in numerous ways, Page acknowledges. But as singleness has become respected and even glamorized, many have been left without sufficient drive to seek a quality relationship and see it all the way through to marriage. "The most important prerequisite for finding a satisfying intimate relationship," Page stresses, "is wanting one. Wholeheartedly, genuinely, earnestly, single-mindedly, and without reservation."[6]

Page has put her finger on a vital and widely overlooked point. We need this single-minded desire to get married because the challenge of finding a good relationship and seeing it through to marriage is so great. We have to take intimidating steps to meet others, deal with rejection, and persist at times when it seems for all the world that one more try isn't worth it. Without an intense desire to be married, we're likely to hold back from taking the risks necessary to win that prize. We'll give up too easily. The dedication to the effort needed to succeed simply won't be there.

Ambivalence not only robs us of sufficient drive to find a mate, but leaves us with *conflicting* drives. When our desire is divided—wanting marriage yet also wanting the special benefits of singleness—we tend to sabotage the very efforts we make to find a partner. Ambivalence about reaching any goal sets us up to work against our attempts to succeed. Most are quite unaware when they fall into self-defeating behavior in relationships, though, and blame bad fortune and a host of unfortunate circumstances for their failures.

Mixed emotions about getting married set us up to be our own worst enemy in our search for a mate. Some end up repeatedly in dead-end relationships, never recognizing the subconscious pattern that's leading them instinctively to choose partners who'll never commit to them. Others find ingenious ways of sabotaging good opportunities to marry, never realizing that their desire to remain single is keeping their desire to marry in place.

Again, Page comments:

> Now, both men and women search for love with one hand and sabotage it with the other. They come to my seminars on how to find love, yet spend the whole day convincing us all that love is restricting. Or they keep themselves too busy to date but then complain about how hard it is to meet people. They dance around relentlessly on the edge of the pool, not willing to dive in and not willing to walk away, get dressed, and forget it.[7]

A Special Problem for Christians

If dancing around at the edge of the pool is an epidemic problem for American singles today, we Christians are certainly more prone to it than anyone. The dramatic social changes affecting singles— the burgeoning singles population and the reinvention of single-ness as an esteemed lifestyle, especially—have had a monumental impact on our churches and the singles culture within them. Thirty-five years ago, you would have been hard-pressed to find a church anywhere in America with a large, dynamic post-college singles group. Today, such groups are so commonplace in metropolitan and suburban churches that you are hard-pressed to find even a smaller city without one.

This exploding singles scene within the Christian community brings unparalleled benefits to those wanting to find someone to marry. If you're 25—or 55—suddenly fellowship groups and activities are nearby where you have a reasonable chance of meeting someone. Chances are greater, too, that others will befriend you, look out for you and introduce you around. There's a natural energy, within the larger groups especially, that works well for those who want to date and meet potential prospects for marriage.

Yet seldom do these groups offer a member *any official help with matchmaking.* Their activities focus much more on promoting singleness as a desirable alternative lifestyle for the Christian than on helping members gain momentum toward getting married. Their events are designed to help members enjoy their singleness and celebrate it, and any coupling that occurs is incidental. While many singles fellowships do sponsor dances, those with minimal dancing skill are left to fend for themselves in navigating the often awkward social climate, or in finding a date for the evening, if they are so fortunate.

Rarely, too, do these groups offer members coaching in social and dating skills, or in steps of self-improvement that will help them be more attractive to the opposite sex, or in strategies for finding someone to marry.

Most unfortunate is the theological understanding of singleness and God's will so often taught and promoted by these groups. It's that God's will for whether you marry or stay single is an objective, not subjective, matter. This is the prevailing idea officially counseled in most singles ministries. God may want you to marry, yes, but may just as likely wish you to remain single—even though you may deeply desire to get married. It's not a matter of your desire, but of his will, and you must wait patiently for him to make his guidance plain. Staying single may be a cross Christ wants you to bear for the sake of his kingdom and the greater work you can accomplish for him unmarried.

Remember, it's stressed, that both Jesus and Paul were single, as were many of Jesus' key disciples, and Paul also speaks pointedly of how staying unmarried brings you many benefits in serving

Christ.

Don't assume, then, that God wants you ever to marry, but let him make that clear to you. It's here, though, that the official teaching gets muddy. Just *how* are you supposed to know what God wants? You're told clearly how *not* to find God's will—that is, through your desires; God's will, in fact, is likely to be the *opposite* of what you desire. But what about *positive* indications of his guidance? Here the clearest teaching you usually hear is, *Don't try too hard to make marriage happen, but let God work it out for you in his own way and time. Let love find you; let marriage find you; leave it in the hands of God.* Christian women, especially, are exhorted to stay passive and always let men initiate. But Christian men also are encouraged not to get too caught up in searching for a mate. Instead, they should focus their energies on doing the Lord's work, and assume that God will make marriage happen for them if he so intends.

The message, then, even though it's seldom clearly stated, is that God will show you through the force of circumstances whether he wants you to marry. If it happens naturally, without heroic effort on your part, and others in the fellowship are favorable, then it's of God. On the other hand, if you're, say, well into your thirties or beyond, and have suffered some rejections, then it's probably time to conclude that God has ordained you to live out your days without a spouse. You'll be happier if you let go of your desire to marry, and make every effort to enjoy singleness and prosper as an unmarried person.

But wait, there's more. Well-intentioned souls who counsel you also not infrequently suggest that God will give you a special sign to indicate whether he wants you to marry or stay single, or whether he wants you to marry a specific person. Countless Christians believe as a matter of deep assumption that God will provide them such a sign, and that they shouldn't marry without it. For those who expect to receive it, then, the special sign trumps the weight of circumstances (even though the latter somehow continue to be important). Rarely, though, does anyone have a clue about what *specifically* this sign will be, or about how to judge its reliability.

Countless Christians have confessed to me that they're deeply frustrated over wanting such a sign but not receiving it. Just as many have confessed discouragement over believing God has given them a sign that they'll marry a certain person, who in fact doesn't want to marry them.

When we look carefully at the biblical teaching on God's will about whether we should marry, we find that it differs markedly from these concepts taught so widely to Christian singles. First and foremost, Scripture stresses that God places within each of us certain deep-seated, prevailing, and longstanding desires, which are a vital indication of the directions he wants us to take with our lives. This motivational thrust differs from one person to another, and is part of God's distinctive fashioning of each of our lives. It's also the primary way he guides the major decisions that most clearly affect our destiny.

David speaks to this point in Psalm 139:13-16, where, in the midst of marveling over God's unique creation of him, he declares, "you created my inmost being". The Hebrew word for "inmost being" is, literally, "kidneys." The Hebrews used this term as we use "heart" today, to speak of one's unique personality and inner life. David, then, is saying that his personality's natural inclinations were implanted in him by God when he fashioned him in the womb, and are a key indication of God's special intentions for his life.

While David speaks of God's placing a motivational pattern in us at birth, Paul speaks of the ongoing nature of this motivation when he notes, in several places, that God "energizes" us. In Philippians 2:12-13, for instance, he declares, "work out your own salvation with fear and trembling; for God is at work in you, both to will and to work for his good pleasure" (RSV). Here Paul notes that God is "at work" in us—literally, *energizing* us (*energeo* in the Greek)—to see that we do what accords with "his good pleasure."

Paul means quite literally that God is motivating and inspiring us to do those things that agree with his special intentions for our life. Because of this, we should take responsibility to make decisions that best reflect the new life Christ has given us ("*work out your own salvation*"), which for each of us is a *distinctive* destiny ("work out your *own* salvation"). And (to complete Paul's circle of thought) we best take that path by following our unique stirrings of heart.

For Paul, then, and for Scripture in general, the most important question we need to answer when taking any major step with our life is, "What is God energizing me to do?" We're nervous with this concept as Christians, because we're well aware that Scripture also stresses the deceitfulness of desire and the importance of self-denial. Yet God wants us to respond to desires differently in major decisions than in minor ones, and it's critical to understand this distinction.

To say it most simply: He gives us deep, enduring desires to signify the major directions he wants us to take, but then expects us to exercise considerable self-denial in carrying out these big choices. By following the paths we most enjoy, we work most energetically and creatively for Christ, and we help others most fully as well. But within these broad commitments, we constantly need to deny ourselves, in order to give our best service to others and to love them most effectively. To the extent God gives us freedom of choice, then, we should base our major choices on what we most clearly want to do, but then be ready to deny our immediate desires often to fulfill these long-range aspirations. Thus Jesus told us to pick up our cross *daily* (Lk 9:23).[8]

I should choose a career, for instance, that I love and long to follow, but then each day exercise all the discipline necessary to carry out my work with excellence and serve others as helpfully as I possibly can.

This same principle applies to choosing marriage or singleness. I should base that choice strongly on what I most want to do, trusting that as I follow my heart, I'll follow God's will. But, if I choose to marry, I should then pick up my cross daily within the marriage, to be the most caring possible companion to my spouse and a godly, loving parent to my children. This is *healthy* self-denial, for I'm exercising it within the context of something I strongly want to do. Neurotic self-denial is choosing to stay single out of duty and (supposedly) service to Christ, even though I really want to be married, for then I'm being unfaithful to how God has fashioned me.

Thus Paul, in his lengthy discussion of marriage and. singleness in 1 Corinthians 7, begins with an umbrella statement: "But since there is so much immorality, each man should have his own wife, and each woman her own husband" (v. 2). By saying "there is so much immorality," Paul notes that the heart wants what it wants, and if you stay single when you instinctively long to marry—as most people wish to do—you'll naturally seek to satisfy that desire outside of marriage in inappropriate ways. Instead, you should avail yourself of the opportunity God gives you to marry. He provides marriage as a gift for your sexual and companionship needs, not because you deserve it but because you *need* it. Paul simply assumes that the great majority of his readers will need this gift, and comes close to commanding them to find someone to marry if, indeed, their need for marriage is strong. Again, "each man should have his own wife, and each woman her own husband."

Paul does make an exception. "I wish that all men were as I am," he exclaims. "But each man has his own gift from God" (1 Cor 7:7). Some, like Paul himself, are blessed by God with a gift of celibacy. They're not consumed with the urge to marry, nor troubled with constant sexual fantasies, but are *content* staying unattached. They are also most effective for Christ unmarried, and Paul joyfully underscores certain benefits that he and others who are naturally energized to stay single enjoy in serving the Lord.

But—make no mistake about it—Paul also recognizes that the overwhelming majority of Christians do not enjoy this gift of celibacy. And never does Paul suggest that those without it should heroically try to stay unmarried, if they have a suitable chance to marry. Staying single then is attempting to live the Christian life in your own strength, rather than in the strength God gives you through marriage.

It is hard to exaggerate the importance of this last point. God puts within us the longing for sexual intimacy and a friendship on the deepest level with someone of the opposite sex. He then makes marriage possible as a means to fulfill this longing, as well as a gateway to countless benefits that make us more productive. He provides marriage *as a gift*, and, like the gift of salvation, blesses us with it not because we're worthy of it, but as his gracious provision for our needs. When Christian singles are told to deny their God-implanted desire for marriage and stay unattached in order to better serve Christ, they're being taught a lifestyle that's nothing short of "justification by works." They're exhorted to be strong morally in a way that ignores God's provision of grace, and forces them to rely much too greatly on their own strength.

The Dilemma for Divorced Christians

Never is the teaching of this misguided notion more tragic than in the case of divorced Christians. They are often advised that God expressly forbids them to remarry. This conclusion is based primarily on four passages in the Gospels where Jesus speaks against divorce, explaining that a divorced person who remarries and his new spouse both commit adultery.[9] Since adultery is clearly forbidden by Scripture, we must conclude that God doesn't permit divorced individuals to marry again, and that he forbids others from marrying someone divorced.

What so many miss, though, is that Jesus isn't speaking directly to divorced people in any of these passages, but to those who are married. He's stressing the exceeding importance of keeping one's marital commitment, and not caving in to the temptation to seek an easy out from the challenges of marriage through the certificate-of-divorce option that the Old Testament law provided. Even more important: he is speaking prior to his crucifixion and resurrection, that is, before his atonement for human sin. In no way whatever does he rule out the possibility that one who is already divorced may seek and find his forgiveness, and through it be in a position to make a new beginning with marriage.

Jesus' teaching on divorce and remarriage must be understood under the umbrella of the central and most important message of the New Testament, that he has died for our sins—that he forgives them, and gives us the opportunity to make fresh starts at those points where we have failed, even miserably. To assume that his atonement isn't strong enough to provide these benefits in the case of divorce is to lessen the efficacy of his sacrifice. It's to declare divorce an *unpardonable* sin, and to grant it greater power in the Christian life than the forgiveness of Christ. That is nothing short of saying that the divorced person who heroically stays unmarried is justified by works in doing so, and not by Christ's atonement.

Yet nowhere does Scripture suggest that divorce is a sin beyond the scope of Christ's forgiveness. Nor does the Bible ever imply that the sinful consequences of divorce are beyond the realm of Christ's transforming power. Never, in other words, does Scripture specifically say that a divorced individual who is truly repentant is forever denied the opportunity to remarry, or can only marry again by committing adultery.

If we understand marriage as a provision of grace from God to help us withstand sexual temptation, then it makes no sense that this benefit would forever be denied to divorced people, who may need it as greatly as anyone else. When Paul declared "it is better to marry than to burn with passion" (1 Cor 7:9), did he suggest that the divorced are an exception to this rule? Did he mean to say that it's okay for them to burn with lust, but not the rest of us? Of course not. That would be tantamount to saying that divorced people must atone for their own sin, and forever turn away from God's gift of grace for their humanness given through marriage.

Divorced Christians who have earnestly sought Christ's forgiveness, have sincerely sought to understand and grow from their mistakes, and have allowed reasonable time to heal, should feel free to remarry. Even more, they should feel free to become proactive in looking for the opportunity. The divorced person may need the benefits of marriage as greatly as the rest of us. If he or she is consumed with sexual need, and beginning to look for inappropriate outlets, that is a sure sign that remarriage is recommended.

If you are shell-shocked, though, from a bad marriage and a difficult divorce, you may find it especially hard to embrace the desire to marry again. You may be more susceptible than most to the ambivalence that deprives you of the drive you need to seek a relationship and move it toward marriage. And to say the obvious: if you believe that God forbids you to remarry, that belief will rob you of what heart you have left to try again. You need to make every effort to understand biblical teaching on divorce from the standpoint of *grace*. As a forgiven Christian, you are under grace, not law. Not only are you free to remarry when the time is right, but there are strong reasons why God may want you to take this step. I look at the biblical issues related to divorce and remarriage in much greater detail in *Should I Get Married?*, and refer you to that discussion if this matter continues to be troubling to you.[10]

I also urge you to seek Christian friends, and a fellowship, who understand and teach the grace-centered perspective of Scripture on remarriage. You need those who treat you compassionately, not judgmentally, in this matter, and who give you every encouragement to take the risk of marriage again once you are ready. While it helps tremendously to know that God permits you to remarry, you'll need great support from the rest of us in finding the heart to do it.

The Heart of the Matter

Whether you're divorced or have never been married, the point simply is that your desire for marriage is *appropriate*. If you find within yourself a strong longing to be married, rest assured that it is God-given, and vital for you to embrace, nurture, and act upon.

Unfortunately, we Christians, in our endless obsession to over-legislate the Christian life, have come up with plenty of reasons to suggest that this desire isn't valid for some of us, nor a relevant sign of God's guidance. Don't let anyone tell you this is so. The message of Scripture, when fully understood, is much more simple and straightforward. God gives us marriage, not because we deserve it, but because we need it. He places the need for marriage in most of us, and intends that we, as a matter of stewardship, make a serious effort to find a suitable opportunity. To that end, he plants the desire for marriage in our hearts, as the single most important sign that we should be open to marrying. He gives us this desire also as a motivating force, to propel us toward finding a partner, and to see a relationship through all its challenges to marriage.

Which brings us back to the point where we began this chapter: Unless your desire for marriage is potent and unobstructed, it isn't likely to give you the emotional steam you need to achieve the goal of getting married. Ambivalence is the greatest enemy standing between you and finding a spouse. In the next chapter, we'll look more closely at what it means to have a desire to marry that is both healthy and strong enough to win the prize.

Five

* * * * * * * * * *

Embracing the Desire
for Marriage

IF AMBIVALENCE ABOUT WANTING TO MARRY CAN KEEP me from getting married, then, what does a healthy desire for marriage really involve? Must I let go of all enjoyment of being single? Must I psych myself up to detest being unmarried?

The answer is a resounding no. God's intention is that we take great pleasure in the life he has made possible for us, *as it is right now*. We should make every effort to enjoy each day to the fullest, in spite of unfulfilled desires. This exhilarating in life in the moment is much of what living victoriously involves. You should strive to enjoy being single, and thank God often for the special benefits of being unmarried.

It is one thing, though, to *enjoy* being single, and quite another to *desire* to be so. There's a major difference, in other words, between making a reasonable effort to be happy for the moment while unmarried, and setting your heart on being so forever. Today we're encouraged to think of singleness as an attractive *alternative* to marriage. In subtle and not so subtle ways, we're advised to plan our life as though we may stay unattached forever. Yet we cannot embrace singleness as even a possible permanent commitment of our life without, by definition, diminishing our desire for marriage. And anything short of an unequivocal desire to be married is probably not enough to fuel the effort we'll need to get there.

When you try to hold on to two conflicting goals, you're not likely to achieve either one effectively. And, invariably, you end up fighting against yourself in attempting to pursue them both. As the proverb says, "If you chase two rabbits, both will get away."

The key is to keep firmly in mind that you intend singleness to be a temporary stage in your life. If you're a college graduate, or attended college for a while, think of your attitude then as a good parallel to setting your heart toward singleness. You enjoyed many aspects of college life, did you not? Yet you clearly understood that period as temporary—as a preparation for a new stage of life to which you strongly aspired. You didn't find it incompatible then to take even great pleasure in being a student, while also cherishing the hope of the day when you would leave college and move on to your career.

In the same way, you can relish the benefits of the single life, while still treasuring the hope of when you can put it behind you for marriage. God has given you the ability to live in both these worlds at once. But holding on to two conflicting *dreams for the future* doesn't work. Imagine the young man in college who yearns for a career yet also longs to remain a perpetual student. He'll likely remain stuck in academia well beyond a reasonable point. And whenever he comes close to leaving college and striking out, he'll be stopped by second thoughts that maybe he isn't ready yet to enter the workforce. "Don't I still need some more training?" His desire for two conflicting lifestyles will make it hard for him to break the inertia of his current, comfortable situation and pursue his other dream. Only a single-minded desire for a career will move him forward.

For so many of us, the challenge of finding a good marriage is

even greater than that of launching a career—and without an unequivocal desire for marriage, the inertia of singleness will probably be too great for us to overcome. It makes sense to examine our
aspirations carefully, and to be certain we haven't unwittingly locked
in to two conflicting dreams.

Why Nurturing This Desire Helps

If God has created you to be married, then the desire for marriage is
already substantial within you—it's fundamental to your personality. If it's not obviously there, then you shouldn't try to conjure it
up—in fact, you cannot. But there's plenty you can do to nurture
this desire, if it's truly present but not providing the motivating force
it should. If you know that deep down you would like to be married, yet also find yourself drawn in certain ways to staying single,
take some time each day to enjoy the dream of being married. Dwell
on what, to you, are the greatest benefits of being in a happy marriage. And consider why, in terms of your life's long-range picture,
a good marriage would benefit you more than perpetual singleness.

You shouldn't think of such fantasizing as psyching yourself
up. Rather, it's a step to let the God-given desire for marriage, which
is already present, emerge and become a more prevailing influence
in your life. Giving this desire more legitimate room to breathe will
help you find the heart to take the often challenging steps toward
finding a spouse.

An earnest desire for marriage will also make you more attractive to someone who would make a good partner for you. Yes, I
recognize that someone may be attracted to you because you *don't*
want to get married. Since he sees you as hard to get, the thrill of
the chase drives him to pursue you. He's the very person, though,
who, once he succeeds in winning your heart, may cave in to commitment fear and run away. Those who fear commitment are typically drawn to partners who are emotionally unavailable. It's
precisely the fact that his girlfriend doesn't want to get married that
gives the commitment-fearful man permission to fall in love with

her. If he deeply fears commitment, though, he'll be quite unaware of his conflicting motives, and will succeed in convincing himself, and very possibly her, that he has finally, once and for all, found the love of his life.

Once she agrees to marry him though, and he suddenly realizes he's locked in, he panics, loses interest, and—often—vanishes.

A strong and transparent desire for marriage will help you ward off the commitment-fearful partner, and will likely save you from many dead-end relationships. It will also make you compellingly attractive to someone who has the potential to commit to you, and who is truly right for you to marry. Think about it from your own end: if you're serious about getting married, don't you want a partner who is equally earnest, even deliriously enthusiastic about getting married? Of course you do—for you know that this person is far more likely to be supportive of you, and to go the second mile in many ways that someone only mildly interested in marriage wouldn't bother. Your own excitement about marriage will likewise be a strong draw to someone who will make a good partner for you, and will help convince that person to marry you.

A clear desire for marriage will also increase the likelihood that friends or coworkers will introduce you to a potential romantic interest. I'm certain more marriages result from such introductions than any other way. If others aren't certain that you want to marry, or that you want help in finding someone, they may hesitate to jump in, out of respect for your privacy. But if you're upfront and eager about it, then they'll feel comfortable playing matchmaker. They'll also be more inspired to help you, and will give more attention to doing so, than if you keep your feelings close to the vest.

Simply telling friends you would like their help, though, isn't likely to make much difference unless they sense you truly want to marry. It's your desire, more than anything else, that will spur them to assist you. It will also give you the heart to gently remind them on occasion that you would love their help, if such a reminder seems appropriate.

Can My Desire for Marriage Be too Strong?
If a strong desire for marriage brings such obvious benefits, though, you may be thinking, what about the other side? Can't this desire also put you at a practical disadvantage? Perhaps you're certain not an ounce of ambivalence resides within you. To the contrary, you've hurt your chances in past relationships precisely because you wanted marriage *so much*. You came on so strong about wanting to marry that you made those you dated uncomfortable. Or, if you haven't caved into such overanxiousness personally, you know those who have scared off many good prospects because of it.

If you're like most of us, you've had a relationship—or an opportunity for one—where you killed your chances by coming on too strong. You wanted badly to win someone's affection, and initially sensed your prospects were good. But you tried so hard that you made her uneasy. You phoned much too often, e-mailed her at the drop of hat, talked too often about getting serious, probed way too much about her past boyfriends. Or in some less tangible way you conveyed that life wouldn't be meaningful without her. She lost respect for you because you seemed so needy, and all your efforts to convince her otherwise only compounded the problem.

It seems all too clear now, with 20-20 hindsight, that if you had just wanted her a bit less, you wouldn't have pushed the envelope in these unproductive ways. You would have relaxed and let things unfold at a reasonable pace. If you had just given her a chance to breathe, she might have discovered that she loved you, and you might have succeeded in winning her hand.

Unless you're very unusual, you have had an episode like this, or at least know others who have. Perhaps pushing these limits has become a pattern for you in relationships. In my young twenties, I drove women in two different relationships nuts with my talk about marriage and my conviction that God had ordained us to be together. (As Christians, our ability to bring God into such discussions as on our side can make our overbearingness even more annoying to the other.)

When we try too hard to make a relationship work, it can seem only too clear that runaway desire is the culprit; it has mushroomed out of control and pushed us into overdrive. But is this really the case? Consider that without intense desire, we never would have sought after this person in the first place! It took strong desire to spur us to break the inertia and pursue this relationship.

In reality, it wasn't our desire that made us unbearable in this case, but our *insecurity*. We let ourselves get too caught up in thinking that life would have no meaning unless this person responded to us. Trust in God to care for us and provide us the right partner was absent. We also lacked a healthy and needed confidence in our own God-given ability to nurture a relationship. And so we panicked, and felt desperate to make this relationship succeed. This fixation made us prone to overdo it at every point, and laid us bare to this person as way too needy.

Fortunately, this problem is solvable. There's much we can do to boost our sense of security in relationships—in fact, doing so is vastly easier than trying to tone down our desire. And with greater confidence, we'll be far less likely to resort to desperation tactics. Addressing these three needs makes all the difference:

1. Strengthen your trust in God. An important part of maturing is embracing dreams and goals with great passion, but at the same time pursuing them with patience and strong trust that God is in control of our life and working continually to bring about his best for us. When we become too needy in our search for marriage, the answer isn't to try to diminish our desire for marriage, but to do whatever possible to increase our faith in Christ.

Taking time each day to be alone with the Lord, to seek his counsel and encouragement, helps enormously, as does regular worship and Bible study. It's just as important to remind myself constantly that God's care and provision for my life extends strongly to this specific area of relationships and the search for marriage. While he expects me to be proactive in seeking marriage, I can do so at a relaxed pace, and trust that he will "give the increase"—

even astoundingly—to my efforts, if he wants a given relationship to succeed. Yes, I may feel some awkwardness in breaking the ice with anyone; but if God intends my success, there will likely be a joyful, natural feel to how things begin to progress. I may even reach the point, and quickly, where I realize I can't do much to keep this relationship from thriving!

On the other hand, if in spite of my best efforts, someone isn't responding to me romantically, I may trust that God has a better option for me. I can let go of any sense that this relationship will only succeed if I make a valiant effort to persuade this person, or resort to heroic tactics. Confidence in Christ means I can move at a relaxed, natural pace in any relationship, trusting that this unde-manding stride ensures my greatest prospect for success. If a relationship simply isn't working, I should face my feelings of disappointment honestly, yet reaffirm my faith in Christ, and my conviction that he is protecting me from an opportunity that wouldn't be best for me.

Most important: Take about five minutes each day (at the be-ginning, if possible) to pray for God's help in finding someone to marry. Ask him to guide and provide for you in your search. Ask him also to give you a gracious spirit toward anyone whom you date or are getting to know. And pray for a heart of trust in Christ so strong that you'll not be inclined to push the limits with anyone. Begin now to make a daily practice of asking for God's assistance, and see what a difference such petitioning can make!

2. Strengthen your dating and life skills. Anything you do to-ward improving your social skills, and other skills that help you feel successful in life, will by definition boost your confidence with the opposite sex, and reduce your need to get desperate. Honing those abilities that help you in searching for someone to marry is, of course, central to this book's concern. So, hang in there—I'll offer plenty of practical advice in the pages ahead. Just keep in mind that growing those qualities and traits that make you most effective in relationships will have the almost magical effect of giving you good *instincts* with someone you're courting. It will become second nature to be patient with this person, even in the face of monumental desire, and to let the relationship unfold at its own natural pace.

3. Strengthen your desire for a strong, healthy marriage. Often, too, when we stubbornly try against all the odds to make a relationship work, our desire for marriage isn't strong enough. You heard me correctly: our desire for marriage in this case is usually too weak, not too intense. I'm speaking here of the desire for a strong, healthy marriage—one that's truly right *for us.* For such a marriage to be possible, we need a partner who naturally loves us for who we are, who doesn't need to be constantly persuaded of our worthiness, nor convinced to be affectionate with us. The thrill of the chase may drive us furiously in certain dating relationships, but it's not the basis for a happy marriage. If you're forced into the beggar role in a relationship, chances are good it will continue in marriage. A good marriage, though, is the opposite of this sad arrangement; companionship rules; you and your partner are instinctively supportive of each other, and neither has to plead for the other's affection.

If you have to make too much effort to win someone's hand, then that person is not likely the one you should marry. You may still feel compelled to make the relationship work because you long for a sense of conquest, or you dread rejection way too much. Or you're so enamored with this person romantically that winning her affection now is far more important to you than the long-term goal of finding a good marriage. It's with good reason that psychologist Judith Sills has termed romantic love "temporary insanity"![11]

The antidote is cherishing hope for the type of marriage that's clearly blessed by God—one where your partner truly is genuinely supportive of you. Focus on the benefits of *this* kind of marriage; do whatever you can to nurture your highest desire for marriage. As *that* passion grows, it will do wonders for your instincts in dating. You'll find the heart to let go of the relationship that simply

isn't working, and be more inclined from the start to pursue someone who'll happily respond to you.

A Special Problem for the Shy Person

The desire for marriage poses a special problem for the seriously
shy person—and a Catch-22. The shy person needs the incentive of
a *very* strong desire for marriage to break through the barrier of fear
and initiate a relationship. He needs this desire also to find the courage to move the discussion toward marriage and finally propose.
Yet this burning desire brings with it the sense that the steps he
must take are *monumental*, and that thought freezes him in his tracks.

It's important to understand precisely what the shy individual
fears. It isn't just rejection. Most of us fear rejection to some extent,
and someone who isn't shy may even have an inordinate fear of
rejection, which seriously hinders her from taking steps of faith.
What the shy person fears most is *her own reaction*. She fears she'll
cave in to panic if she breaks the ice—that she'll fall apart, become
tongue-tied, faint, and make an utter fool of herself. This fear of
self-mortification is nothing short of a phobia, and one that far too
often keeps her from doing what she deeply wants to do.

Of course, the shy person fears rejection as well, though in a
more morbid sense than most do. He not only fears someone he
asks out will turn him down, but that she'll laugh at him and ridi-
cule him, and that others will find out and consider him a loser for
even trying.

I understand this shy mentality well, for I've struggled with it
throughout my life. I was so shy as a young teenager that, when I
first set my heart on asking a certain woman out, it took me five
months to muster the courage to do it. When I finally did ask her,
her response couldn't have been more positive, and we began a
dating relationship that lasted over a year. Yet I shutter to think of
how I came so close to not making that one phone call that finally
erased my fears.

My personal odyssey with shyness has also given me profound

appreciation for what really works in confronting the problem. I can say wholeheartedly, from 45 years as a Christian, that the shy person benefits exceedingly from a growing relationship with Christ and a deepening trust in him. Learning social and dating skills helps as well, as does the encouragement and support of friends, and professional counseling sometimes brings benefit too. But as with conquering any phobia, at some point you must simply push through your apprehensions and do the very thing you dread, to finally tame your fears. Shy individuals too often think they must first fully overcome their fear before getting socially active, but this process isn't psychologically possible. It is *action* that finally subdues your fear, and nothing else can substitute.

I'll look at how you can learn to stare fear down and find the courage to break the ice in relationships at different points in this book. Here, I simply want to assure you that this is a most achievable goal. Shyness brings with it issues to confront, but it doesn't have to defeat you in your search for a mate. Take heart that being shy can actually *help* you in winning another's affection, and work for you in many ways. You shy temperament will be endearing to the person God wants you to marry; it makes you a good listener, and usually a better one than the less shy person is. You're also far less likely to be aggressive in annoying ways. God has given you your temperament for good purposes, and it will bring you many advantages once you move beyond your fears and seek to build a relationship.

Here is perhaps the best news: Anything you do to increase your desire for marriage will help you to overcome your shyness. Yes, there is the Catch-22: greater desire can bring with it greater apprehension about taking initiative. Yet the truth is that the intensity of your fear will not grow as greatly as the intensity of your desire. The remarkable fact is that at some point *desire trumps fear!!!* If you want marriage badly enough, you'll find the courage to break through the inertia of fear and take the risks that now seem unthinkable. Truly, nothing will help you more in smashing fear's barrier than deepening your passion to be married. So don't repress that desire, but nurture it—by focusing on the benefits of marriage, and by praying that God will both deepen this desire in your heart, and meet it wonderfully as you pursue your dream to be married.

And remind yourself often of this incredible fact of human nature: that desire triumphs over fear—and that specifically, the desire for marriage, when it's strong enough, will give you the push you need to move forward.

Your Heart's Desire Is Your Ally

To return to the main point of these past two chapters: desire also trumps ambivalence. And the corollary: without a strong, clear, and undivided longing to be married, you won't likely take the steps that will lead to marriage, even if you're not at all shy. Even worse, if desire isn't sufficient, you'll likely, in subtle and subconsciously-driven ways, sabotage the efforts you do make to find a partner.

Yes, a golden opportunity to marry sometimes finds the one who isn't looking for it, and who may even be doing everything possible to avoid it. Such fairy tale experiences are the stuff of Hollywood scripts. They're the staple, too, of certain pastors and notable Christian speakers, who love to stress how they were simply about the business of doing the Lord's work, not looking for marriage at all, when the chance to marry suddenly caught them by surprise.

What they fail to appreciate is that it was precisely because they were in the public eye so much that this "surprise" occurred. They were in a far better position than most to meet potential partners, for prospects to take initiative with them, and for others to play matchmaker. It's tragic when such leaders imply (as they too often do) that their experience—of staying passive and just letting marriage find them—should be the norm for all serious Christians. It's even more tragic when single Christians take this advice to heart and try to follow it (as happens way too often).

In truth, it's no more likely that most of us will find marriage through passivity than that we'll find a good job this way. God expects us to take the same sort of earnest initiative in seeking a spouse that we take in building our career—this is his normal intention for how most of us will move toward marriage. And because finding a mate usually involves plenty of trial and error, we need nothing short of a burning desire for marriage to encourage us on. It's to this end that God himself plants this desire within us. If he wants you to be married, he has given you a deep, intense desire to marry—it's already a major part of your temperament. Your need is to focus on it, affirm it, and let it fully emerge.

Let this desire take its natural place on the front burner of your heart. That is the most important step you can take toward finding someone to marry.

Six

* * * * * * * * * *

Optimism and Expectancy

MY GRANDFATHER MET HIS WIFE IN A WAY YOU'LL NOT find recommended in any dating manual.

He arrested her.

While on duty one morning in 1920, Washington patrolman Sgt. Milton D. Smith stopped a motorcar on Dupont Circle for exceeding the 18-miles-an-hour speed limit. He intended to take the driver to the station and cite her. Kitty Horton, though, was apologetic, and my granddad softened. He gave her a lecture about safe driving instead, and told her he would keep an eye on her.

That he did.

As he reflected on this chance encounter, he felt Kitty was someone he would like to get to know. He had her address from the traffic stop, and so he called on her. The rest is history. A relationship blossomed, they married and lived happily together for the next 30 years, until his death in 1950 at 64.

My granddad's experience highlights the single most encouraging part of looking for someone to marry. It's that finding the love of our life can happen suddenly, unexpectedly, on any given day, as we're about our normal routine, in the most unlikely circumstances. We should take heart from this fact often, and let it give us hope as we start each day—for the day we're entering is unlike all others and may bring with it the new beginning for which we're longing.

Yet it also reminds us of the importance of being alert to the golden opportunity when it comes along, and ready to act on it. Which brings us to the critical need for a positive, expectant attitude when searching for someone to marry. Unfortunately, this is where so many of us lose the battle before it begins, for without an optimistic spirit, that believes success is possible for us—even likely—we may fail to recognize a splendid opportunity that's staring us in the face. Or, if we do sense its presence, we may lack the heart to act on it, fearing our chance for success isn't great enough to justify the risk.

My grandfather had plenty of reason not to be expecting anything unusual that morning when he pulled over Kitty's car. His first wife had died tragically about a year before, in the flu epidemic of 1919, when she was just 26. His grief over this great loss could easily have overwhelmed him and kept him from seeing the chance for a new beginning. He was also in full police mode when he stopped Kitty. He saw her as a reckless driver disrespectful of the traffic code, and felt responsible to treat her as such. It must have taken quite a paradigm shift, and a quick one, to see her from a different viewpoint, and to recognize that God might have something *for him* in this situation.

It also must have taken a special kind of courage to break the ice and let her know he was interested in her. It meant letting go of his police authority, swallowing his pride, and laying himself vulnerable to someone he barely knew. The risk was huge, for had she responded negatively, he not only would have felt rejected as a suitor, but ashamed he had let down his professional guard.

Then there was a reason my granddad could have assumed his

prospects with women in general were poor, and that trying to win at love wasn't worth it. At five feet, two inches, he was the shortest policeman on the D.C. force. Men commonly think of height as a special benefit in courting, and many regard shortness as a disability. Not my grandfather. His small stature was a mark of pride to him. And he determined to present himself as the most courageous, effective possible officer in spite of any limitation of his size. He succeeded so well in this mission that he caught the attention of local news writers, who featured many articles on his exploits in city papers.[12]

His is an inspiring example of how a limitation—or a perceived one—can be turned into a strength. In reality, any personal feature or circumstance that we think of as a limitation in relationships can be a strength if we *view* it as such—for self-esteem itself is sexy, endearing, and makes us compellingly attractive to others. It's a matter of focusing on the positive side of "the hand we're dealt," and expecting the best in the opportunities life presents.

My grandfather demonstrates so well this sort of positive, bold spirit that can make all the difference for each of us in our own search for mate. I urge you to strive for this kind of attitude, and to do whatever possible to keep your heart encouraged, optimistic and hopeful about succeeding. Without this buoyant outlook, your prospects for finding someone are dimmed, for negative thinking shuts you down, keeps you from seeing possibilities, and robs you of the energy to take initiative. Unfortunately, negative thinking is far more natural to most of us than positive. We each have had enough experience of rejection, and suffer enough instinctive fear of failure, that we're programmed to a certain extent—more than we probably realize—to *expect* failure. Yet when we give in to gloomy expectations, our eyes fail to open to opportunities in front of us, and the momentum we need to seize them fails to take hold.

How do you lock in to this positive attitude? There's the rub, you will say; you've tried positive thinking, but it's never worked! Indeed, most of us have gone through maddening episodes of trying to psych ourselves up to think positively, perhaps thinking initially we succeeded, only to find that the slightest setback throws us back to square one. Despite the claims of countless self-help books, you can't simply will yourself to think positively; you can't just choose to do it. The human personality doesn't work that way.

Your mind *is* amazingly capable of lifting you out of discouragement and into a spirit of optimism, though, *if* you work with the natural way it functions. The most important thing to understand—and it's not complicated—is that God has designed your mind *to think*. It cannot simply be told what to believe, but needs to be convinced. The more deep-thinking and analytical you are, the more fully this dynamic is true. You are capable of great optimism about your future; yet your mind needs persuasive reasons for the hope it embraces.

No matter who you are, there are substantial reasons why marriage is a good prospect for you, providing you take sensible, practical steps toward finding someone. Yet you need to dwell on these reasons, call them to mind often, and allow your mind significant opportunity to embrace them. Equally important is to clearly identify the reasons why you're discouraged or fearful or expecting the worst, and then carefully dispute the basis for your gloomy perspective. You should reason through your negative thoughts, in other words, and challenge them at every point where you're overreacting.

Let's say as an example that you would like to ask a woman to dinner whom you've recently met at the gym. She's been friendly to you, and as best as you know, she's not attached. Yet you fear strongly she'll turn you down if you ask her. You're just as anxious that this experience of rejection, if it does occur, will be too devastating for you to handle.

Your fear and negative assumptions will easily prevent you from testing the waters with your new acquaintance. Here's where carefully examining your negative assumptions and disputing them can get you over the hurdle. Remind yourself first of all that you have no solid evidence she'll reject you. Even if you've been rejected by others before, she is someone different who may see you through a different lens. Remind yourself, too, that success sometimes surprises us happily when we take a bold risk. Call to mind examples that prove this point. Recall specific times when you expected a certain step would fail, but you went ahead anyway—and succeeded! Think of similar experiences your friends have had, in relationships and other areas. Enjoy these memories and dwell on them.

Then consider the worst-case scenario if, God forbid, it should occur. What if she makes it clear she doesn't want to date you? Are there possible benefits to this happening? You bet there are! One is that you'll then be free to stop obsessing about her and move on to other possibilities. And she may not be the right person for you at all; her turning you down may be God's protection from a bad relationship, and his way of preserving you for someone better. Asking her out will allow you to clear the air and to determine if the potential for a good relationship is there.

Challenge also your assumption that you'll fall apart if she declines your invitation. The truth is, God has made you resilient and far more capable of standing up to rejection than you think. Yes, you'll feel disappointed; yet you'll also feel good that you didn't cave in to fear but, instead, took a bold step. Undoubtedly, too, you'll learn from the experience and will be better prepared for the next opportunity to ask someone out.

Countering negative assumptions with thoughts like these is profoundly mood-altering, and can give you the extra edge you need emotionally to take risks. Your mind, though, needs some generous opportunity to do this therapeutic reasoning. Spend a few minutes at the beginning of each day focusing on all the reasons you have for hope that you'll find someone wonderful to marry, and challenging your negative thinking wherever it needs disputing.

Then make a practice throughout the day of reminding yourself, as often as you need to, of the reasons for hope that you recognized so convincingly during your reflective time, and continue to dispute negative assumptions and fears that keep troubling you.

With practice, this sort of focused, practical meditation can re-shape your perspective into a vibrantly optimistic one. Like main-taining physical health, though, this attitude transformation takes effort and maintenance. If you find yourself losing your hold on an optimistic spirit, don't get discouraged about *that*, but simply do what's necessary to restore it. Your mind *will* cooperate; thinking positively and hopefully is as fundamental to how it functions as the will to live. With practice, this positive attitude will become more consistent and begin to reap countless benefits for you.

Let's look more specifically at the real-life particulars of dating and seeking a marriage partner where this attitude makes all the difference. There are at least five occasions when it's vital.

1. To recognize the golden opportunity when it comes along. Stop and think about it. Every successful relationship begins at a moment in time when someone perceives it might be *possible*. It's this initial recognition of the possibility that sets everything else in motion. Yet unless one believes she has a respectable chance of finding a good relationship, she'll not likely conclude a certain acquaintance might be interested in her. That moment of perceiving the possibility simply won't ignite unless her attitude is optimistic and expectant.

Even in the face of an excellent opportunity, this perception of the possibility is often a hair's breadth matter—a delicate moment that just barely makes the cut. A man considers asking out a certain woman, for instance, who will in fact respond positively to him. As he muses about it, he concludes his chance of succeeding with her is just a little greater than his chance of failing. If his attitude is only slightly less positive, he'll perceive these odds as reversed, and con-clude the effort isn't worthwhile. His optimism needs to be strong enough to get him to the tipping point where he feels initiative is justified.

And, as my grandfather's experience demonstrates, the golden opportunity sometimes presents itself briefly and unexpectedly—

and so it takes an especially alert, expectant spirit to recognize it. He had plenty of reason just to move on to the next traffic stop that day, and not to give a second thought to his brief encounter with Kitty. It took eyes of faith to see it as a divinely-given new beginning for him.

Even when an opportunity presents itself blatantly and repeatedly, we may still fail to perceive it if our expectations are negative. I recall a time when I was directing a musical group in the 70s, and a female member grew interested in a male member, who was also clearly attracted to her. She signified her interest time and again in ways that, while always appropriate, were quite obvious to me— by giving him that extra measure of attention and affirmation. Yet he never asked her out or made the effort to convert their friendship into something more. Years later I asked him about it (they are now both happily married to others), simply curious why he had never responded to her. He was stunned when I mentioned she had been interested in him romantically, insisting he had never recognized it. In hindsight, I'm certain the conviction a relationship with her wasn't possible kept him from reading the signals.

Whether the special opportunity presents itself subtly or blatantly, anything we do to keep our attitude positive and expectant will increase the chance we'll recognize it. And it will best ensure we'll have good judgment about how to break the ice.

2. To be *ready* for the special opportunity. It's just as important to be ready for the special opportunity, and by that I mean to be presenting your very best self at that moment when you need to do so. Someone is most likely to take interest in you if you're optimistic they will. Your optimism draws them in, makes them feel comfortable with you, and causes them to sense you have something special to contribute to their world—for optimism itself is contagious. Optimism also positions you to give the right cues through your body language—brightness in your composure, good eye contact, a warm smile, an open stance.

If you suspect someone won't like you, on the other hand, that assumption becomes a self-fulfilling prophecy, for you instinctively do things that drive that person away. Your rigid body language conveys that you expect the other to dislike you, and leaves him or her uncomfortable warming up to you. And when you expect rejection—believe it or not—you have a certain investment in proving to yourself and others that you're correct. You like having your negative assumptions validated. So you may do certain things, even subtly and unconsciously, that sabotage a good opportunity.

Of course, *some* nervousness about rejection is normal in the face of a new opportunity, and won't hurt your chances, as long as you don't allow it to control you. The key is to focus as much as possible on the positives—especially on your hope for success and the reasons why it's possible.

Focusing on the possibility of meeting someone, as you begin each day or enter a new situation, and believing it may happen, also makes it most likely you'll *dress* in a way that will help you in that setting. I strongly recommend making it your lifestyle to dress and groom daily as if you'll meet the love of your life on that day. Do I mean that when you wake up blurry-eyed on Saturday morning, with no particular agenda, that you should shower, shave, fix your hair nicely, use a light fragrance, and put on something other than your cleanest dirty shirt? Yes. Absolutely. Consider that if you knew for certain someone would knock on your door at 11:00 that morning collecting for cancer research, that you would strike up a conversation, invite her in for lunch, and that this chance encounter would spiral into the wonderful relationship you're looking for— you would look your very best for that occasion, would you not?

The truth is, this sudden, unexpected opportunity may occur for you at some point, if not from a knock on your door, then when you're at the grocery store or pharmacy or mall, perhaps, or walking your dog in the neighborhood. Looking your best will increase your chance for success when the unexpected happens. Your pleasant appearance not only will draw the other's interest, but good grooming will boost your self-esteem and help you convey a positive spirit at that moment.

So we're talking about a positive cycle here. Positive expectations for the day lead to looking your best, and good grooming boosts your mood as well. Of course, you can overdo it. You shouldn't wear black tie when taking your pet ferret to the vet. Dress for the occasion, of course—just dress as though you know you'll meet your future spouse on that occasion. Follow the dictates of your heart in terms of how you present yourself. Just remember that keeping your heart hopeful and optimistic about meeting someone will best ensure you have good judgment about grooming and dress. This positive attitude will *cause* you to look attractive as well. Two vital reasons why optimism will help you be ready for that golden moment when it comes.

3. To work through mixed signals in a relationship's early stage. We would like to think that when a great relationship opportunity is unfolding to us, a sixteen-foot angel will suddenly appear holding a huge neon sign, flashing the message: *"This is the one God has ordained for you. Marry her!!!!!"*

In reality, the signs we have to go on at this time are usually much less spectacular. They include this person's friendliness, and subtle indications of interest he or she may convey. Often, too, we seem to be dealing with *mixed* signals at such a time; she seems unusually friendly toward us in certain ways but not in others, for instance. It's critical at this stage to habitually question our negative assumptions, for they're often inaccurate, and may too quickly cause us to think we're being rejected when that's the last thing on the other's mind.

When my friend Maggie Whall was a freshman at University of Maryland, a young man whom she immediately liked sat next to her one day in Organic Chemistry. And because he was friendly and politely flirtatious, Maggie thought he might be interested in her. Jeff continued to be just as amiable whenever he sat next to her on the days after that. Yet on some days, Jeff chose to sit a row or two behind Maggie, even though she kept a desk open next to hers.

Maggie came close to concluding Jeff's random seating pattern showed he really wasn't attracted to her. She even feared he might be making an intentional statement so that she wouldn't get her hopes up.

Yet Maggie was astute enough to question her negative assumptions, and to realize there might be another explanation for where Jeff decided to sit. One day, when he chose a desk behind her in spite of an empty one beside hers, she simply asked him pointedly if he didn't like sitting next to her. Maggie's bold, nothing-ventured-nothing-gained spirit paid off unspeakably for her. And for Jeff. For he responded that, yes, he *did* like sitting next to her, but he was left-handed and needed a left-handed desk.

Oh.

From that day on, Maggie arrived a bit early to class and made certain a left-handed desk was positioned next to hers. Today, she and Jeff are very happily married with three children of their own in college.

Theirs is an outstanding example to keep in mind if you ever feel you're getting mixed signals from someone who strikes your interest. If she seems to be saying "come close, go away," it's worth paying more attention to "come close," at least initially. Remember, you don't know this person well, and "go away" may have an explanation you don't yet understand that has nothing to do with rejecting you. Learning to dispute your negative assumptions at this time can make every difference in preserving a good opportunity and letting her have the chance to prove herself. Again, it's all about priming your heart each day to expect the best and not the worst in relationships, then staying open-minded when someone's initial signals are confusing.

4. To work through futility about taking initiative to find a relationship. If ambivalence about getting married is your greatest barrier in searching for a mate, futility is a close second. Futility is the sinking feeling that a certain step you *can* take toward meeting someone can't possibly work for you. You've been disappointed so often with this approach that you're certain history will keep re-peating itself if you try again.

Fear is also a hindrance to your success, though it's not as for-midable as futility. When fear is your enemy, you believe you may succeed, but you're afraid of the consequences if you fail. Yet be-cause fear stares you in the face, you recognize it and have the chance to address it head-on and conquer it. Futility is effective in shutting you down precisely because you *don't* recognize it. You truly believe you're seeing the world realistically: your premise that your past defines your future is certainly correct, and so obviously your chance for success is nil. What you don't recognize is that it's really depression talking, and that what you're taking for reality is anything but.

In truth, most of us find the love of our life through taking a step that has failed for us before. Indeed, most of us find our spouse by taking a step that has failed *many times* previously. You trudge to the singles meeting 100 Sunday nights in succession without meeting anyone who interests you. But on the 101st visit you strike up a conversation with a newcomer who turns out to be your prince. Or well-meaning friends set you up with blind dates from the abyss no less than 15 times—but on their 16th try finally get it right. Or you drop in on the swing dance time after time without anything igniting with anyone, yet then comes that extraordinary night when you leave singing "Some Enchanted Evening."

This isn't to say you shouldn't make strategic decisions to change your circumstances in order to improve your prospects for meeting someone. You absolutely should. The time may come when you need to leave that ingrown singles group that hasn't seen a new-comer in three years, for the larger, more dynamic group with a constant flow of visitors. The point simply is that, no matter where you chose to roost, it may take many visits before something sig-nificant happens. Futility is your worst enemy in this case, for you may grow convinced it's not written in the stars for you to prosper in this setting—even when success is just a visit away. Keeping your life in motion is critical. And always, *any action is better than none*, for by placing yourself in a pubic setting—any setting—you position yourself for things to happen that won't if you're sitting home alone.

A friend of mine lost his wife to cancer. Her death was devastating to Eric, who had been happily married to Linda for 33 years.

A year or so later, Eric began dating Janet. He quickly fell for her and hoped they would marry. Janet wasn't so sure. After two years of dating, Eric hadn't wavered in his desire to marry Janet, yet she hadn't moved beyond her ambivalence. Eric, now in his mid-fifties and eager to marry again, felt he had to get on with his life, and so he broke up with Janet. Once again, he was heartbroken over a major personal loss.

A short time after their breakup, Eric agreed to attend a concert with a friend. He stopped by a bookstore to purchase an album by the band that was to perform, to be better prepared to enjoy their concert. While there, he ran into a young coworker of his. She introduced Eric to her mom, Shirley, who was shopping with her. Eric chatted with Shirley for a few minutes—long enough to find she had lost her husband to heart disease several years before.

A week later, Eric asked Shirley out. They quickly found they were highly compatible, and began seeing each other frequently.

Eric, who had every reason to think God had abandoned him, benefited greatly from staying active and hopeful about life. His decision to make the concert experience as positive as possible led to his visiting the bookstore, which opened the chance to meet Shirley. His experience reminds us that doing something, no matter how mundane, is far better than doing nothing.

I should add that Eric, who is an avid reader, had shopped at this bookstore and others on countless occasions without anything so unusual happening. Yet this time a stunning opportunity broke through. This is a great example of why staying in motion is so important, for happy surprises can occur at any time and in the most unlikely settings. Yet you need a strongly positive spirit to fight through futility and find the heart to keep trying. Again, we're re-minded of the immense benefit of this attitude, and of striving to stay encouraged and hopeful as we search for a mate.

5. To let go of the relationship that isn't working. It's impor-tant to stay highly optimistic about winning someone's heart when you first become interested. You don't know him well, and so even if he's attracted to you, you may misread his signals and take a positive indication negatively. So it's vital to question your nega-tive assumptions at first, and to earnestly test the waters. And even if he isn't interested in you initially, your positive spirit may win him over.

Unless she clearly tells you she's already spoken for, or plainly says she doesn't want to date you, you shouldn't take her first no as permanent. Waiting a week or two and trying again is justified, and probably another time after that. If she's attracted to you, or has any potential to be, reasonable persistence on your part will be endear-ing to her—and it may make the difference.

The operative word here, though, is *reasonable*. You cross a line, sometimes fairly quickly, where persisting and staying hope-ful about someone works against your long-term goal of getting married. This may sound like I'm contradicting myself. Haven't I been urging you to stay optimistic about your prospects as you search for a mate, even if the odds seem great? Yes, definitely. But it's optimism *about getting married* that's most important—that is, be-lieving you'll find someone wonderful who wants to marry you. Staying hopeful about *that* dream is highly justified. A given per-son who attracts you in the process may or may not respond to you. If she doesn't show interest after a reasonable effort on your part, then the most positive thing you can do is move on. You need strong faith at this time, to believe God has someone better for you and doesn't want you to bog down in an unfruitful situation.

It's all too easy to get stuck at this stage, even if someone has told you no repeatedly. Heartsick longing to win her affection can keep you trying and trying again, and stubbornness can as well.

You may also have a certain comfort zone with this person by now, and it may seem easier to keep asking her out than to strike out and try your fortune with someone new. But letting your heart stay tied up with her will rob you of the time and energy you need to find one who truly will respond to you. In the worst case, she may even sense you're stalking her, and take stern action to get you to stop.

The more determined and hopeful you are about getting married, the easier it will be to turn away from the hoped-for relationship that isn't working, and "cut your losses."

You need this positive spirit as well to turn away from the relationship that *is* working well in certain ways but doesn't show good potential for marriage. You may date someone who loves and cherishes you and is pleased to be your boyfriend, but who plainly says he doesn't want to marry you. Or he may take way too long to decide, or commit to marry you yet then cave in to commitment fear and vacillate. It's so important to think clearly at such times and to keep your dream of getting married firmly in mind. If, in all honesty, you know he'll not likely commit to marry you, you need to break your ties with him, in order to find someone who will. A determined, optimistic spirit about getting married is vital to finding the heart to break off the wonderful relationship without marriage potential, as this step is often the most heart-wrenching one you have to take en route to finding your mate.

Of course, the hardest part about letting go of the dream of marrying someone is dealing with feelings of rejection. Even if she isn't rejecting you as a friend or a romantic partner, she is rejecting your dream of getting married, and so your sense of loss can be overwhelming. And you may experience more blatant rejection at times: someone tells you plainly that he doesn't want to date you, or breaks off a dating relationship after giving you strong reason to think he'll stay committed to you. Rejection is life's most painful experience; a single episode can send you back to the dugout, resolved you won't chance the experience again. And the simple fear of it can block you from even trying in the first place.

A healthy attitude toward rejection is so critical in your journey toward marriage, and so vital to the positive spirit you need to succeed, that I want to devote a chapter to it now. Looking back, you often realize that rejection was an amazing benefit, for it cleared away one option to allow an even better one in. But without a resilient attitude toward rejection, you may not stay in the race long enough to make this discovery. Let's look carefully now at what this attitude involves.

Seven

* * * * * * * * * *

Dealing with Rejection

"I'VE SPENT TWO WEEKS CRYING OVER LOSING HIM."

So Louise described to me her reaction to being shelved by Harold. Louise is not a self-pitying person, but a mature, vivacious individual. Yet she was much less prepared for what happened than she thought. She had let her hopes get too high about a future with Harold, and not without good reason. He had said he was open to the possibility of a serious relationship. But after several months, he decided that their differences on certain spiritual issues were too great. They would do best to forgo getting serious but stay friends.

Friends? Small comfort to someone who had marriage in mind.

Many people falsely imagine they are invulnerable to the hurt of rejection. I remember thinking as a new Christian that believers must be fairly well insulated against major heartbreak. I was to find in time that my humanity remained well intact. You may have likewise imagined that your spiritual perspective or life philosophy would protect you from the pain of rejection, but then were devastated when it actually occurred. It's something even the most stout-hearted among us discovers: rejection cuts deep.

Let's look at why rejection hits us so hard, but most importantly, at how we can better prepare for it—and even benefit from it. We come now to a matter that isn't as pleasant to think about or anticipate as others we're considering. Yet it's an area of experience that's just as essential to understand and be ready for if you are to realize your goal of finding a lifetime companion. The fact is that you will probably go through at least one episode of rejection or disappointment on the way to meeting the person you marry.

I originally considered titling this chapter "Accepting the Inevitability of Rejection." I decided against that because it's too negative and connotes a sense of fatalism about rejection that I don't mean to imply. I intend this book to boost your hopes, not diminish them!

Still, that title does capture something of what I want to say. If you are to stay strongly hopeful about finding a partner, you have to be steeled for the sort of experiences that too easily squash your dreams. Far too often, a single occasion of rejection is enough to do it. For many, too, the mere fear of the possibility of rejection keeps them from moving off square one. In either case, the reaction is much more extreme than warranted. Indeed, rejection, rightly understood and handled, can take you closer to your goal of marriage rather than further away. It's not the ultimate catastrophe we make it out to be.

The truth is I don't know any happily married person who didn't suffer at least one major disappointment before finding the person who was right for her or him. Most went through several unhappy episodes prior to meeting their spouse. It's not that this absolutely has to be the case. Yet it doesn't seem that God exempts many of us from this pattern.

None of these people will deny that the pain of these disappointments was considerable. Yet most will also admit now that even their most difficult relationship experiences of the past brought them certain benefits. These incidents not only helped prepare them for the realities of marriage, but sometimes in ironic ways brought them closer to meeting the person who became their lifemate.

Seeing Rejection's Positive Side

With the right perspective, it's possible not just to survive rejection or the unhappy ending of a relationship but to actually benefit from the experience. It all has to do with your perception. Typically, when disappointment occurs in romance, we are prone to three unfortunate conclusions:

"I am unlovable." I don't have the right qualities for someone to love me in a marriage-quality way.

"God doesn't want me to be married." He has shown me through this closed door that he wills for me to stay single.

"I won't be able to love again." The one person whom I truly loved is not available. It wouldn't be genuine to expect I could feel this same intensity of love for another person.

Each of these conclusions is unnecessary and tragic: unnecessary, in that it doesn't likely reflect the reality of our life as God sees it; tragic, in that if it persists, it too easily becomes a self-fulfilling prophecy. Let's look more closely at why these assumptions are so detrimental.

I Am Unlovable

We are instinctively prone as humans to reason from the specific to the general. When the emotional intensity of an experience is great, we tend to view the rest of our life through the eyes of this one experience. Yet the conclusions we draw can be most misleading.

It isn't exaggerating to say that the death of expectations for a relationship can be as heartbreaking as the physical death of a loved one, especially when you've placed great hope in these anticipations being realized. In *Coming Apart*, family therapist Daphne Rose Kingma suggests that the ending of a relationship of short duration can be even more painful than the demise of a long-term one, for you've had less chance to see the other's imperfections and thus to have some basis for seeing value in the breakup.[13] Of course, the failure of a relationship even to get off the ground can be devastating if your hopes have run high. The rejection of a single date can crush you.

In the wake of any such experience of loss, grief you suffer must be felt and worked through. It's normal to feel at a low point then and to dwell on your disappointment. At this time, though, while not denying your feelings of disappointment, you should make every effort to remind yourself that this relationship was but one among an almost infinite variety of possible others for you, and that it doesn't have to mirror your future. In the immensely complex world of romantic relationships, where the chemistry doesn't take in one case, it takes wonderfully and surprisingly in another. There are so many intangible and unpredictable factors involved in what draws two people together that you never have a basis for concluding that all hope for finding a good relationship is gone.

Beyond this is the very important fact that you can often learn valuable lessons from a failed relationship that will improve your prospects for finding an enduring one. I say this cautiously, for it isn't always true that you can learn clear lessons from past failures, and you must be careful not to self-flagellate in the process. My advice is to look only for very obvious lessons that are there.

In my own case, for instance, I learned through two difficult experiences as a young single that women found me insensitive when I spoke too soon about my thoughts on God's will for us. I told them early in the relationship that I thought he wanted us to be married. As I came to understand how presumptuous I was in doing this, I determined to change the pattern. It allowed for a much more relaxed and spontaneous relationship with Evie.

Let me caution you, though, to avoid resolutely the thought that things might have turned out better if you had acted differently. There simply is no way to know this. Here you need to rest fully in the grace and protective hand of God, and trust that he has your very best in mind in what you've gone through. Even if you had done everything perfectly, the breakup might still have occurred. As painfully academic as the thought may seem at this time, the day may come when you thank God from your heart that things transpired as they did. When you've met the right person, the relationship will work in spite of many weaknesses and imperfections on your part.

In any case, don't fall into the trap of predicting your future on the basis of your past. Your past experience in relationships in no way proves what your future will be. Someone else may respond to you very differently. Don't write history before it happens!

God Doesn't Want Me to Be Married

When we suffer romantic disappointment, we tend to reason outward from that one experience to what broader message God might be giving us about our life in general. Too often the conclusion is negative: God is showing me through this roadblock that I should stop pinning my hopes on getting married and should face the reality that he wants me to stay single.

Seldom, though, is this conclusion justified. When St. Paul addresses how to set your heart concerning marriage in 1 Corinthians 7, he simply says that you should plan on getting married if your need is strong. Obviously, he realized some of his readers didn't immediately have a prospective spouse, and that some had been rebuffed in their efforts to find one. Yet never does he remotely suggest that the lack of present opportunity, nor any number of failures, should be taken as God's telling you not to plan on getting married.

Quite the contrary, he even says that widows should look toward getting married again if their need for marriage remains strong (1 Cor 7:8-9, 1 Tim 5:14-15). I doubt that anyone is more inclined to conclude God doesn't want them married than one who has suffered the death of a spouse. Yet Paul allows no room for such a fatalistic assumption. Underneath it all, his attitude is supremely optimistic.

Why, then, does God allow us to experience disappointment in relationships if the reason isn't to show us we should stay single?

One very important reason is to keep us from entanglements that wouldn't be good for us. In his infinite knowledge of the future, God sees much more clearly than we possibly can whether a particular relationship would result in a healthy marriage and contribute to his best intentions for our life. "There is a way that seems right . . . but in the end it leads to death" (Prov 14:12). Sometimes the only way God can protect us from the romantic equivalent of driving off a cliff is by bringing about the breakup of a relationship we cherish. Only with time and hindsight do we appreciate his wisdom.

Another reason is to teach us lessons about life and relationships that can only be learned through experience. Also, difficulties build tenacity and resilience into us that can only be acquired through experience. Such events bring us back more fully to trusting him to meet our deepest needs.

Finally, but not least significantly, a more mystical factor is involved that can often be demonstrated but never fully explained. There seems to be a law in human life that a certain number of failures are sometimes required to bring about a success. To say it differently, success sometimes comes only through a number of earnest attempts. It's the principle of seed bearing talked about so frequently in Scripture. Some seeds take root while others don't, for reasons we never fully understand. Yet the greater the number sown, the greater the likelihood of a rich harvest.

Thus Ecclesiastes:

> As you do not know the path of the wind, or how the body is formed in a mother's womb, so you cannot understand the work of God, the Maker of all things. Sow your seed in the morning, and at evening let not your hands be idle, for you do not know which will succeed, whether this or that, or whether both will do equally well. (Eccles 11:5-6)

When disappointment comes in romance, out tendency is to think that failure once means failure forever. We see the lots cast against us, and imagine ourselves living an isolated, lonely life. Yet the principle of seed bearing suggests that an experience of failure may indicate that we're now in line for a success as much as anything. Success isn't less likely now, but more so! If we'll simply keep casting the seeds, eventually one will take root.

It's fair to think of this, too, as a principle of compensation. Failure with one try is compensated for by success at another. All of this adds up to one important point: There is purpose in trying again when you experience disappointment or rejection in a relationship. You must not close the door in this or any area of your life before God is ready to do so.

I Won't Be Able to Love Again

Even if you accept that you might be successful in another effort, though, you may find it hard to imagine that your feelings of love can redirect to someone else. Hasn't God so created us that we're capable of experiencing full-fledged romantic love for only one person in a lifetime?

As pervasive and deep-seated as this notion is, it hits wide of the mark of reality. In fact, God has so constructed the human psyche that any individual can experience the feeling of romantic love toward a potentially large number of people. He has put within each of us an extreme measure of resilience. It's to this end that Paul tells the widow she "is free to marry anyone she *wishes*" (1 Cor 7:39, emphasis added). Clearly underlying this statement is the assumption that the widow will be *able* to love again. If this is true for someone whose spouse has died, it certainly can be true for one who has suffered a broken relationship.

It's noteworthy that Boaz is Ruth's *second* husband, her first having died in Moab. Ruth is once again able to invest her romantic energy in a relationship. It's in the book of Ruth, too, that God is described as "a restorer of life" (Ruth 4:15 RSV). This is a vital concept of God to keep in mind in the face of disappointment. He is a God who heals, and a significant part of his healing work involves enabling rejected individuals to find new directions for their affection. Thus, the psalmist's remarkable description: "A father to the fatherless, a defender of widows, is God in his holy dwelling. God sets the lonely in families" (Ps 68:5-6). And: "He gives the barren woman a home, making her the joyous mother of children" (Ps 113:9 RSV).

This isn't meant to minimize the pain we may experience in rejection. But it is to say that light is at the end of tunnel. Over time, we can overcome the pain and redirect our romantic affection.

I experienced these feelings of rejection strongly when a church friend told me politely but firmly that she wasn't interested in dating me. I had let my hopes for a relationship with her get out of hand and now felt quite deflated. I confided in a pastor, who advised me that, while I shouldn't ignore my feelings of disappointment, I should move as quickly as possible to find a new place for my affection.

He expressed the point in symbolic terms: "If you have a glass filled with dirty water, there are two ways to get it out of the glass. You can dump it out, in which case the dirty water is quickly gone but the glass is left empty. Or you can take a pitcher of clean, cool water and begin pouring it into the glass. Gradually, the fresh water will displace the dirty."

He went on to explain that the empty glass represents the unhealthy way of dealing with a broken relationship: bailing out of life, turning off your emotions, turning a hard heart to the possibility of new relationships. Pouring fresh water in the glass represents the healthy approach: You admit your feelings of regret, which are only too real, while at the same time taking steps to build new social contacts. Gradually, the new life that comes from them will take the place of the anguish that now seems so overpowering.

His advice proved sound. Within a week, I found the courage to ask out another woman in our church's college group, and the experience rejuvenated me. My hurt feelings continued to gnaw at me for some time. But new friendships, and eventually marriage itself, brought substantial healing. Even today, it's possible to jog myself back into the feelings of that hoped-for relationship of more than forty years ago. But I can also say with gratitude that I'm glad now it didn't work out.

Symbols are important to us, and I believe you will find the metaphor of the pitcher and the glass a helpful one to keep in mind in the face of disappointment in relationships or any other area. God has built great resilience into each of us. We are much more capable of rebounding from rejection and failure than we may realize. Yet an important process is involved, and this analogy describes it as well as any elaborate explanation could. Don't let the inertia of life overtake you when things don't turn out as you had hoped. Break that inertia, seek new relationships and new outlets for your energy, and let the cool, fresh water fill the glass.

Rejection, while always an unpleasant experience, doesn't have to be a catastrophic one. Indeed, when rightly handled, it can be a positive step toward your goal of finding a lasting relationship. "And we know that in all things God works for the good of those who love him, who have been called according to his purpose" (Rom 8:28). "All things" includes rejections and unwanted endings to relationships. Even in these he is working out a plan that has your very best in mind. Dwell on that as you seek his courage to move forward.

Eight

* * * * * * * * * *

Doing What Doesn't Come Naturally

I MET A MAN AT A PARTY RECENTLY WHO, BECAUSE HE'S also a writer, took an interest in my work. When I told him I'm writing a book to help singles find a spouse, Pete replied that some of his friends could definitely use it. He went on to explain that he has no less than five close male friends in their 40s and 50s who dearly want to be married but have long been stuck in neutral. Each is successful professionally, a good friend to Pete, and a wonderful person in his own way. And each has much to bring to the table in a good marriage. Yet none has ever enjoyed a serious relationship with a woman, and most haven't dated in ages.

The problem, Pete explained, is that none is willing to make any personal changes that might improve his prospects. Each assumes that the right woman will simply accept and love him as he is—baggy jeans, dirty sneakers, three-day overgrowth, and all. None believes he should strive at all to sharpen his appearance, to improve his communication skills, or to better understand what a woman wants and conform to it—for efforts like these would be unnatural, insincere, and beside the point. Each cherishes the notion that he is *already* Mr. Wonderful, and that the right woman, when she finally comes along, will instinctively recognize it.

Yet each is pushing midlife without any successes to prove his theory.

I was surprised by Pete's story—but only by the sheer number of close friends he has who simply don't get it when it comes to relating to women, for the problem he described is epidemic among single men today. Not a few women fall into this pattern as well.

But then Pete stunned me with a story of someone else close to him who *did* get it. His own father. By the time his dad died at 48, he had been married . . . *ten times*. Each marriage lasted only a year or two and then broke up over his dad's struggle with alcoholism, which is what eventually took his life. Yet in spite of severe personal problems, this man managed to work his way into a woman's heart, convince her to marry him, then see the relationship through to marriage, on an astounding ten occasions. Whatever the negatives in his example—which are plenty—there's a positive that deserves our highest respect. It's that this man had an extraordinary gift for relating to women and inspiring them to want a serious relationship with him.

It's the contrast between Pete's dad and his five friends that I find most interesting, for their examples represent two extremes common today among those who want to get married. At one are those who succeed outrageously in relationships, and seem to without even trying. They may not win every heart they set out to conquer. But more often than not they do. They instinctively know how to enter the other's world and make that person feel important, cherished and supported. And they present themselves in a way that makes that person want a deeper relationship with them. Like Pete's dad, such relationship succeeders may have plenty going against them—even serious personal problems. But they manage to do certain things brilliantly right that contribute to their success in romance.

The fact that such people succeed, sometimes in spite of serious personal shortcomings, is inspiring, for it shows that you don't have to get everything right to win someone's affection. You can learn certain relationship shills and make certain changes that will greatly improve your chances; but you don't have to be a picture-perfect human being, nor do you have to sacrifice being yourself at the most important levels. I urge you to observe these relationship succeeders, for you can learn much from them. And their examples, taken in the right spirit, can give you fresh heart to keep trying, and to reinvent yourself in ways that will help you succeed with the opposite sex.

At the other extreme, Pete's friends remind us that some who long to be married are their own worst enemies. They have certain fatal flaws that keep them from building close relationships. Most tragically, they fail to recognize how they're shooting themselves in the foot, nor to appreciate any need for self-improvement. At worst, they think of themselves as God's gift to the other sex. At best, they feel it's insincere to make any changes that might help them succeed. They assume the love of their life will accept them for who they are; she'll instantly recognize and cherish their hidden strengths, find their rough edges endearing, and fit in with their life as comfortably as their pet golden retriever. She'll find her own needs wonderfully met simply by logging time with such marvelous specimens of humanity and basking in their aura.

The irony is that these same individuals, who resist change when it comes to relationships, have usually striven greatly to improve themselves in other areas. They may have devoted years to education to learn certain skills or a whole new trade. And they've likely adapted to their chosen profession's culture in countless ways in order to succeed (make no mistake about it: dressing down on an IT job is as much an acquiescence to culture as dressing up at a law firm). They are different persons in professional life than before they took on their career; they've reinvented themselves in many ways. They've likely done so in other social contexts too, perhaps in relation to a club, church, or association to which they belong.

Still, they'll say, relationships should be different. After all, our closest friends and family members love us without reservation and cherish our company even if we haven't bathed in several days or brushed our teeth in a while. We should expect our life partner, of all people, to do the same.

Yet is it really true that our best friendships and family relationships blossom spontaneously without any effort on our part? When you think back carefully, you usually find that you adjusted plenty along the way to accommodate these people and fit into their worlds. Each relationship has been, in its own way, a growth experience for you, and you've allowed yourself to change in different ways that have helped it prosper. It's just that you've now hit such a comfortable stride with these people that it's easy to forget past challenges. You can probably think also of good friendships and family relationships that have soured because you weren't willing to bend enough.

Yes, I'll grant you may have had that occasional friendship that for ages has worked remarkably well in spite of everything rough-edged and ill-natured about you. No matter how you search the past, it's hard to remember any way you've personally changed or altered your lifestyle to better meet this person's needs (though to call your friend long-suffering may be an understatement).

Still, in *marriage* you're joining forces with someone in the most intimate, enduring, and time-intensive friendship forged with anyone in your earthly pilgrimage. Of all friendships and human contacts you enjoy, there will likely be a learning curve and a growth process to qualify for this prize. Yes, this person will treasure you for who you are in the most important ways. Yet *who* you are is not a purely static thing; both nature *and* nurture are always involved, and your personal uniqueness evolves over time.

Being Your Best Self

To find our soul mate and win this person's heart for life, each of us needs to hit a happy medium. We need to recognize, on the one hand, that God has given us a certain individuality from birth that is basic to his intentions for our life. It shouldn't be changed, and doesn't need to be in order to find a marriage partner. We have certain tastes, preferences, interests, gifts and abilities, and ingrained physical characteristics, that are fundamental to who we are and to what makes us beautiful as a person. At the same time, none of us lives in isolation. From the earliest age, we're thrust into a world of people and relationships where, if we're to succeed socially, we have to modify our behavior in certain ways, grow in our ability to communicate, and—if we're to enjoy the richest of human bonds—learn to reach out in compassion to others' needs. Most of us will find that about fifty-percent of what we need to do comes naturally, but the other half requires learning, growth, and experience.

When it comes to forging an intimate friendship for marriage, what might you need to change in order to succeed, and what should you leave alone? Here, a simple consideration of the golden rule can be a revelation. Imagine someone you know whom you would consider marrying. It's clear enough she has a certain uniqueness—an individuality you don't want her to alter just to please you. But . . . you also want her to be attentive to you and considerate toward you in certain ways, don't you?

Let's say you've asked her out for a first date, and arranged to meet her at a restaurant at 6:00 p.m. You would like her to arrive on time, maybe a couple of minutes early. If she phones at 6:10 to say she's lost, it's not the unpardonable sin; but it's unsettling that she didn't take more care with directions and *a little* insulting to you. If she shows up at 6:30 without a compelling reason for her tardiness and a heartfelt apology, it's close to a deal killer.

Then during your time together that evening, you hope she'll focus on you. It would be nice if she turns off her cell phone. While you would like her to talk about herself and share interesting details, you hope even more that she'll show interest *in you*, and ask pertinent questions that help you open up—then be a good listener who is genuinely interested in your responses. You hope too that when you probe about her life, she'll not be evasive but will give you meaningful replies. It would mean the world, too, if she's complimentary to you for small things throughout the evening.

You also hope she'll look nice. Among the multitude of ways she might dress, fix her hair and groom, you would like to see that it's *important* to her to present herself well to you. You also want her to have impeccable hygiene.

Her body language will also convey volumes to you. When she arrives, it would mean so much if she initiates a light kiss and hug. Then you would like her to *look* interested in you throughout the evening—to maintain eye contact, to ignore her watch and cell phone, to lean toward you often, to smile frequently and naturally, and to touch you lightly on the hand or arm from time to time. At the end of the date, a kiss and a warm hug that she initiates, or gratefully accepts from you, will make your day.

Turning the tables further: If your time together isn't a restaurant date initiated by you but a dinner at her home suggested by her, then you'll have certain further hopes that she'll either meet or disappoint. You would like to find her house is nicely kept, and that she shows you gracious hospitality. You also hope she takes care to fix a meal she knows you'll enjoy, and prepares it well. Especially, you hope she wants you to linger afterward, and that she offers dessert, beverage and snacks fit for the occasion.

You also hope that as your evening draws to a close, she'll show earnestness about seeing you again soon. And if she commits to contact you by phone or e-mail, it's vital she carries through.

Now consider that we've noted about a dozen ways in which you hope your friend won't merely be herself when she's with you this evening, but her *best* self. Of course she could, in the name of being herself, slough off at any of these points and treat you less than considerately. Even if she cares for you greatly in spite of such rough-edgedness, you would find it harder to believe she does, and would feel less motivated to pursue the relationship further. You want her to be herself, yes—but you also want her to strive to be a good companion to you in each of these ways. As long as she doesn't overdo it absurdly, you don't view this considerateness as violating her individuality, but enhancing it.

Now apply the golden rule: what would it require for you to treat her as you want her to treat you? And why is this effort any less important on your part than hers?

Hopefully this simple mental twist makes it easier to see that some effort may be needed to weave yourself into this woman's heart, and that making it doesn't mean you've stopped being yourself. It is, rather, part of the unavoidable dynamics of building a serious relationship. Doing *only* what comes naturally may not work for you. It doesn't work for most of us. Most of us find that some work and focus is involved, if we're going to win the most prized of human relationships. And there's usually a learning curve; most of us have some growing to do. We may need to develop deeper sensitivity to the needs of the opposite sex, improve our communication skills, learn to better navigate social expectations in dating and courting, and make other personal changes that help us succeed.

As elementary as this point may be to many of you, it may surprise others that I'm stressing it, given this book's topic. My theme is that most us do best to marry someone with whom we enjoy a strong bond of friendship—and that this friendship has much more to do with our happiness and success in marriage than romance and other factors society glorifies in love relationships. I'm also stressing that this means less pressure as we look for someone to marry and grow a relationship, for it's easier to build one on a foundation of friendship than romance, and easier to find someone open to one with us in the first place.

This doesn't mean the pressure is off completely, though. You may still need to grow and change in certain ways, to be in the best position to attract a friend to such a relationship and to see it through to marriage. And some watchfulness will be needed through the whole process—it won't all be purely natural.

And now perhaps the biggest surprise of all. The fact that you're seeking to marry a friend doesn't mean you can let go of all concern for the romantic. Here again the golden rule. By this point in our study I hope you're appreciating that friendship is the most essential core of a happy and successful marriage. Yet even if you're embracing this outlook, you still have certain romantic and sexual needs you're hoping marriage will meet. Even if they aren't on the same pedestal now, you can't dispense with them entirely—and you shouldn't. They are part of the drive God uses to draw you into marriage, and an essential part of what makes the marriage relationship different from all others. Your partner, like you, is also cherishing the hope of enjoying physical intimacy in marriage.

And so, no matter how magnificent your friendship, simply being good buddies with your partner will probably not be enough to carry you down the aisle; you also need to respect his needs for romance. It's vital to stand in his shoes and appreciate his expectations about marriage and courting. Like you, he's been programmed from the earliest age to expect certain benefits in marriage, and to expect a certain process leading up to it. These expectations are probably negotiable to some extent, but not fully dispensable.

If you're a man deeply desiring marriage, but wanting a friend who'll just accept you as you are, realize that no matter how extraordinary a friend your wife will be, she has a side that wants to be treated as a sweetheart, that wants to be courted. It's vital to appreciate her feminine side, and to realize she not only wants to be esteemed as a friend, but as a woman. Dressing and grooming in a way that respects her, being a gentleman in every possible way, being expressive about your love for her, affirming her often, adding romantic touches (flowers, candlelight dinners), and, more often than not, letting her be right in discussions—such things may be critical your success.

If you're a woman longing for a husband, but hoping he'll accept you in exactly the way your female friends do, realize he has been programmed from birth to want femininity in a spouse. And he hopes for a level of sensitivity and compassion from you that his male friends don't provide. It's exhilarating to him, and flattering, if you give special attention to your hairstyle, wear a new dress that you've bought just for this special date, use a fragrance he likes, touch him lovingly, and make it a habit to be flirtatious with him.

This attention to the romantic doesn't need to be obsessive. And you shouldn't let it be. If it becomes the overriding concern of so many relationships, it will stress you out and interfere with your most important mission, which is developing friendship. Think of tweaking the romantic as the frosting on the cake (to use the horribly trite metaphor, but it does make the point). Think of it also as showing compassion to your partner, by helping meet this person's deep-seated needs for romance and intimacy. Taken in that spirit, it fits perfectly with growing the supreme friendship of your life.

Do unto Others (Whom You're Courting) . . .

Effective courting, to a large degree, boils down to common sense—once you open yourself to it—and to the golden rule. Please keep in mind constantly that winning someone's hand in marriage may require some changes in how you relate to the other sex, and in grooming and hygiene too. Ask yourself seriously, how do I wish someone I'm interested in to treat me and to care for their appearance? Then, make every effort to treat this person similarly, and just as royally.

If you want further help with relationship skills, numerous books are available, and I recommend browsing the relationship section of your nearest Barnes and Noble for an ever-evolving selection. If you find communicating with the opposite sex difficult, no book offers more practical help and insight than Debra Tannen's *You Just Don't Understand: Women and Men in Conversation*.[14] In a compelling, readable style, this Georgetown University linguist explores the often baffling differences in how we communicate between the genders, and does so better than anyone who has written on the subject. Hers is one book I can say assuredly will increase your understanding of the other sex, deepen your empathy, and help you communicate more effectively and confidently. And, of course, countless books are available on improving dating skills and navigating a serious relationship. Nearly every one has something to offer. You will do well, in fact, to read as much as you can, but especially to draw on those books that boost your hope and confidence in seeking a marriage partner.

I will return to the subject of dating skills in chapter 14, and look in greater detail at how you can best present yourself and best treat your partner in the early stage of a dating or courting relationship. My *main* concern in this book is to help you find someone to marry and to recognize golden opportunities that can easily elude you. This is where I believe this book will make the greatest contribution to your search for a spouse, and help you in ways that most others on this topic won't. So for now, as we move on to look more directly at strategies for finding a mate, I simply ask you to keep this timeless truth in mind: whatever qualities you want in the friend you marry, *being* this sort of friend is the most important step you can take toward winning that person's heart.

Part Three

* * * * * * * * * *

Finding a Special Friend to Marry

Nine

* * * * * * * * * *

Seeing the Treasure You Already Have

IN DECEMBER 1965, I TOOK A STEP THAT I KNEW WOULD forever change my life spiritually. I had no inkling—not the remotest clue—how it would drastically reshape my life in every other way, especially socially.

For sometime I had been listening to the radio broadcasts of Dr. Richard Halverson, pastor of Bethesda's Fourth Presbyterian Church. Something he said in a sermon on Sunday evening, December 5, penetrated my shell so effectively that I knew it was time to drop all defenses and commit my life to Christ. About 11:30 the next morning, after attending classes at Georgetown University, I climbed into my car and began driving around nearby streets. In the privacy of this mobile sanctuary, I prayed earnestly, telling God I wished to give my life to Jesus Christ, and that I intended my decision to be permanent—a lifetime commitment.

My spiritual quest leading to this decisive moment was unusual in that it took place privately, with no one counseling me or cheering me on. While driving one Sunday evening the previous summer, I had unintentionally caught Dr. Halverson on the radio. I was so moved by his sermon, which I listened to entirely, that whenever I was free on a Sunday evening after that, I went for a drive at 8:00 p.m. and tuned in his broadcast. Yet I told no one about my intrigue with his messages, nor about the convictions growing within me. So on that December day when I accepted Christ, I wasn't trying to impress anyone or win their approval, nor did I expect any social benefits to result. Those benefits I did expect were purely spiritual—a richer relationship with God, and the blessing of his guidance in my life. The possibility that my social life might suddenly transform simply wasn't on my mind.

It's here that I was in for huge surprises.

I hesitated to attend church at first, not comfortable walking into a congregation of strangers. Yet on Christmas morning, I felt compelled to go, and so I ventured to Fourth Presbyterian, just a ten-minute drive from my home. Folks were friendly enough that I decided to return on Sunday—the next day—for the church's regular service. Afterwards, a woman sitting several rows behind me called my name. I spun around to find it was Melissa Burns, who dated the organist from my band, the Newports.

The Newports were a rock band I directed, which largely defined who I was then. I had begun playing guitar in seventh grade and had launched my first band, the Galaxies, that year with several classmates. In spite of our tender age, the Galaxies soon began playing for dances. In my tenth-grade year, 1961, the Galaxies morphed into the Newports, and I grew obsessed with developing a top popular band. Now, in my junior year of college, the Newports were playing constantly and had logged over 500 gigs.

My hope from the start was that playing in a band would help me socially, and boost my appeal to women. That goal largely failed. Most women who interested me didn't want to hang out at band jobs, and band work left me little time for a social life. I envied the Newports' organist for having this wonderful girlfriend who was willing to accompany him to our events. I didn't know Melissa well, though; and she knew me mainly as a rowdy performer, who drank way too much before, during, and after gigs.

So on that Sunday morning, she was as stunned to see me in church as I was to encounter her there. We stayed in the sanctuary for a few minutes and chatted. I explained that I had recently become a Christian, and told her how Dr. Halverson's radio preaching had affected me. Astonished, she insisted I attend the college Sunday School class with her, held downstairs the next hour. I followed her to that room, where she introduced me around. Then, during an open prayer time, she prayed very audibly, "Thank you, Lord, that absolutely anyone is welcome here."

The ice was now so thoroughly broken that I began attending the church's services regularly, along with their college activities, which were numerous. Because Melissa was my best friend there initially, I frequently stopped by her home, to talk about my new spiritual journey and goings-on at church. A young neighbor and church friend of Melissa's, ninth grader Evie Kirkland, often popped over when I was there. She and Melissa were good friends, and Evie enjoyed hanging out at her home. Evie was intrigued with my band experiences and my unlikely conversion to Christ, and I enjoyed her attention. Yet she was merely a junior high kid to me then, and nothing more.

In the months that followed, something remarkable happened that I neither intended nor expected: My life thoroughly transformed socially. In February 1966, I quit the Newports, opening up much more time for a social life. Fourth Presbyterian had a large and growing college fellowship that met frequently for activities, and I began attending everything. I was warmly accepted as a new Christian, made many new friends, and quickly gained a new identity having little to do with the Newports.

The most extraordinary change for me personally—and the most welcome—was that women in this group were more open to dating me. Within a year, I enjoyed two short-term dating relationships, and then a third began that lasted over a year. These boosted my self-esteem and confidence with women tremendously.

The downside was I grew *too* confident. I became too choosy about whom I dated, and too drawn to a woman's flashiness. My audacity set me up for some humbling experiences. On one occasion, I grew convinced God wanted me to marry a certain woman in the college fellowship. And so I told her. To my dismay, she replied that God hadn't directed her in any such way, and that she wanted no more than a friendship with me.

Then I went through a similar episode with another woman. I believed God had given me a revelation about marrying her, and . . . well, you know by now how that story goes.

And so my experience with women at Fourth Presbyterian was an evolving one, with some welcome highs and mortifying lows.

One other evolution took place for me during this time, and it was a gigantic change involving music. My sabbatical from it didn't last long. Several months after leaving the Newports, Fourth's youth director persuaded me to organize a Christian band to perform at the church's college events. The result was Sons of Thunder—a fledgling group of volunteers at first, but within a year, a talented ensemble. Sons of Thunder became as serious an endeavor for me as the Newports had been, though with a vastly different mission and audience. Students at church began inviting us to perform at their colleges, and with that momentum, we started playing full-time in June 1972.

By now I was 26. I had graduated from Georgetown in 1968, then attended seminary locally for four years and had just graduated. Evie Kirkland (remember her—Melissa's ninth-grade friend?) had just finished her junior college year. I had seen her often at Church over these years, and we always got along well. She was my second-oldest friend there, yet I still thought of her as a younger sister.

That summer, though, we began chatting more at church events. She seemed like a peer now, not a youngster, and the age difference no longer significant. Evie had time on her hands that summer and volunteered to help with Sons of Thunder office work, which was overwhelming me. Her assistance was invaluable. And working together strengthened our friendship—which soon would become the most important of my life. Then one evening we began kissing in the band's office; our friendship had taken a romantic turn.

That fall Evie returned to college in North Carolina for her senior year, but we phoned and corresponded, and she found her way to several Sons of Thunder concerts in the south. During winter break, we began dating seriously. Then that April, 1973, I asked her to marry me, she accepted, and we held our wedding five months later, on September 8.

It's now 37 years later, and every day has been a confirmation of God's goodness in bringing us together, and of our decision to marry. I've never lost my intrigue, either, with the chain of events that led to our first meeting at Melissa Burn's home when I was 19, and then to my change in perspective many years later—when I realized that here before my eyes was the woman I should marry.

Your Dream Within Reach?

I've shared this personal odyssey with you, with all its twists and turns, in the hopes it may provide some inspiration to you in your own search for someone to marry. It offers several lessons that many, as I did, discover by default in their journey to marriage. The most interesting is that the person you marry so often ends up being someone you've known for a while but haven't considered seriously as a lifemate.

I knew Evie Kirkland solely as a younger friend for six and a half years before a serious relationship ignited. This was also a period in my twenties when my dating life was the most fertile and my hope to find someone to marry strongest. Yet never did it cross my mind during this time that Evie might be God's choice for me. It was as though a veil was over my eyes then. The situation, of course, was similar for her: she was eager to find a husband, and dated different men during that period, but never thought of me as a possibility until that summer of 1972.

Our situation was somewhat unusual in that I had overlooked Evie because of our age difference, which became far less significant as we moved into our twenties. Yet our experience was similar to many others' who marry a longtime friend, in that we had known each other for many years and shared some important common history. We had both long been active at Fourth Presbyterian, and Evie had enthusiastically followed the development of Sons of Thunder, now such a major part of my life. But while our friendship was fueled by strong points of common experience, a romantic relationship hadn't been part of it.

This past week, legendary television personality and pitchman Ed McMahon died. McMahon was renowned, as you may recall, for those countless Publishers Clearing House ads in which he proclaimed: "You may already have won a million dollars!" It's here, at this point in our study, that I want to announce just as exuberantly: "You may already know the person whom you should marry!" You may, in fact, know this individual *well*. But it's just as possible that you've never considered this friend as a possible mate.

But wait, there's more.

It's here that I want to encourage you to give some serious attention to taking inventory of your relationships with the opposite sex. I urge you to set aside some generous, focused time to consider if someone you've overlooked, among past and present acquaintances, is your ideal match. If you've ever taken inventory of your personal assets, I'll bet you were surprised by some encouraging discoveries. You probably came across certain items you had long forgotten you owned, and found that certain possessions were more valuable than you realized. Was there an unexpected treasure among them? Just recently I discovered that an old, beat-up guitar I thought was nearly worthless is actually valued at $4,000 on the collectors market. Such unearthing of hidden treasure is common when inventorying our possessions.

It's just as common when inventorying our relationships. We

would like to think we're masters of all the important information affecting our lives, especially that which comes from our own experience. Above all, when it comes to the people we know, we would like to imagine we clearly recognize all the possible ways we might relate to them. Yet we each have many blind spots. Simple discouragement and negative thinking can shield us from recognizing new social opportunities. Inertia limits us greatly as well; we don't naturally imagine that a relationship we've categorized in a certain way might suddenly be able to take on a very different nature. The inventorying process focuses our mind, and compels us to see the full picture of what we have—with possessions or relationships—and opens our mind to new possibilities. Done properly, it can open us more fully to God's inspiration, and help us grasp his bigger picture for our life—which is the best part!

But if that's true, how then do we inventory relationships in a way that brings such benefits? The most important thing is to give some liberal time to doing it. I recommend taking a personal retreat, and devoting an afternoon or (preferably) a day or more to the process.

Of course, by now you may find that your inspiration process is already engaged enough that you don't need special effort to nurture it. The mere suggestion of taking inventory of your friendships, or that marrying a friend is a good idea, quickly brings to mind a dear friend whom you suddenly see in a new light. Such an epiphany can happen anywhere, anytime, and isn't limited to a personal retreat. Or you may already have been waking up to the possibility that someone you've neglected is your ideal mate.

But, if by this point in our study you're drawn to the idea of marrying a friend but don't see any obvious option on the horizon, a personal retreat may help you think more deeply. It may be a time of happy surprise, when you suddenly see the potential in a friendship you've never considered in light of marriage. It can also be an excellent occasion to reflect more fully on whether to marry someone you're currently considering.

God's Inspiration

In the next chapter, I'll provide some guidelines for taking a personal retreat. Before going further, though, let me say something about the nature of the inspiration you may experience during such a time. What you're endeavoring to do is to give your mind greater freedom to think broadly about your options. On a deeper and more profound level, though, you're opening yourself to the inspiration of God—and it's here that things can get confusing. How do you distinguish between the voice of God and your own wishful thinking? While it's unlikely you will hear God's *audible* voice, it's possible you will have a sudden insight or epiphany so dramatic and surprising that it seems God has spoken to you.

I understand both the possibilities and the peril of this experience well. One of those incidents I mentioned when I misread God's will for a relationship occurred on a personal retreat. On a balmy July afternoon when I was 25, I ventured to nearby Sugar Loaf Mountain for a time of prayer and reflection. After walking to the summit, I sat on a rock overlooking the beautiful farmland of rural Montgomery County. There I thought about the future and prayed for God's direction. Within a few minutes, I was overcome with the sensation that God wanted me to marry a certain woman in our church's college fellowship, whom I neither knew well nor had felt romantically attracted to before. I genuinely believed I had experienced a revelation from God about my future with her.

Eventually, I ramped up my courage and asked her out, and we dated several times. Although she gave no indication of interest in getting serious with me, I decided to go ahead and share my "vision" with her. After all, I believed God has privileged me with a revelation affecting both our futures. She responded that her sense of God's will was quite different from mine, and she wasn't interested in marrying me nor, at that point, in dating me further. The experience, to say the least, was deeply humiliating and discouraging to me.

On another occasion, though, my experience with a personal

retreat was much more rewarding. In early January 1973, I spent a couple of days praying and reflecting in solitude at a camp in Mt. Airy, Maryland. This was during the period when things were growing serious with Evie. At one point during this retreat time, I had a sudden moment of conviction, where I envisioned Evie and me married—and it felt right in every way. As I pondered that inspiration, doubts I had been harboring seemed to melt way. I felt that God was moving me to propose to her, and that on the deepest level, this was what I most wanted to do.

This time I finally got it right! But why, then, did I succeed so well in understanding God's guidance on this occasion, when I failed so miserably on Sugar Loaf Mountain? The truth is, I didn't fail completely then. I believe I was right to ask out that woman, whom I'll call Betty, and that God prompted me to do *that*. But I read far too much into his guidance and let my expectations soar unreasonably, and that's where my problems began.

I carried an assumption then about how God guides that was simply wrong, and it set me up for disappointment with Betty—though I still succeeded on a certain level. Let me suggest three principles for understanding God's inspiration, which will help you avoid my mistake yet be open to the insight God truly provides you. This will also allow me to further explain my experience with Betty.

The first principle is the most important: Normally, when God guides us, his purpose is to prompt us to do something, but not to reveal what the results will be. He doesn't unveil our future to us, in other words, but merely nudges us to take certain action. And he gives us the insight we need to take that step—*but no more than that*. His guidance isn't a crystal ball. We always remain dependent on him for further guidance, which only comes as we move forward.

The psalmist, speaking of God's communication with him, declares, "thy word is a light unto my feet, and a lamp unto my path" (Ps 119:105 KJV). Think about it. If you walk through the woods on a dark evening with a light in your hand (a torch when the psalm was written, a flashlight today), it illumines just the space right in front of you, giving you only enough light for your next step. You have to take it before you can see clearly for the step beyond.

This is a perfect metaphor to God's guidance. He gives us just enough insight for the next step ahead of us, but no more. We always have to take that step to be in position to understand God's direction for the one that comes next. Rarely, if ever, does he reveal with certainty what our personal future holds, nor guarantee what the outcome of a certain action will be. He wants us to stay fully dependent upon him as we move forward. If we knew very much about our future, the basis for walking in faith and trusting God for continued guidance would vanish, along with much of the adventure of walking with Christ.

We humans, though, are prone to read more into God's guidance than is justified. When God moves us to do something specific, we may feel highly encouraged that he has enlightened us and enabled us to be decisive. That elation is legitimate. In it, though, it's an easy jump to fantasize about the outcome of our action, and to be so overcome with hope for a certain result that we assume God is assuring it to us. We're especially susceptible to this projecting in romantic relationships, where hope and desire can run extraordinarily strong. And so if God gives us light unto our path for a relationship—he inspires us to take a step to get to know someone better, for instance—we take it as a searchlight scanning out our future and revealing our destiny. While God has prompted us merely to take certain action, we believe he's guaranteed the results.

This is the mistake I made when praying on Sugar Loaf Mountain. In hindsight, I truly believe God prompted me that afternoon to ask Betty out. He gave me light unto my path about the relationship. But I took it as the searchlight. I immediately began to muse about what marriage might be like with her. And I enjoyed the fantasy so much—with the very limited information I had then—that I assumed God was revealing the relationship's future. Even worse, I shared my presumed vision with her, putting her in a highly uncomfortable position. Instead, I should have simply let the relationship unfold, trusting that if God wanted us married, he would reveal it step by step, and as clearly to her as to me.

Which brings me to the second principle for understanding God's guidance. It's that when he guides us, he influences not only our emotions but *our mind*. He gives us *reasons* for what he wants us to do. He helps us understand why taking certain action *makes sense*. He blesses us with *wisdom* about our choice, to use the Old Testament term. We may *feel* inspired, yes, but more important, we suddenly are able to think more clearly. When a decision we're considering is based on something less than clear thinking and solid wisdom, we have reason to question whether God is guiding us. At the least, we should ask him to provide us with a clear reason for taking the step.

My inspiration on the mountain about marrying Betty went way beyond any logical basis I had for thinking it could happen, for I scarcely knew her. She had been friendly to me a few times at church events, and so asking her out and testing the waters was justified. I had reason to conclude God was prompting me to do that—but nothing more, and no guarantee whatever about the outcome.

On that personal retreat when I felt prompted to propose to Evie, on the other hand, the situation was very different. In that case, I had a number of strong reasons to believe marrying her made sense, and that she would probably say yes if I asked her. I was able to think these reasons through carefully, and to work through some doubts as well—to the point that I felt a surge of confidence that proposing was the right thing to do. But that moment of inspiration was based on solid evidence.

This is the real value of the personal retreat: it allows God—who gave us our mind in the first place—to influence it and enable us to think more broadly and effectively, to the point that we may experience a strong conviction about what to do.

The third principle related to God's guidance is that we always benefit by following God's prompting, even when the immediate results don't turn out as we had hoped. God is good, and he does not guide us capriciously. If we've made a sincere effort to understand his guidance, and base our choice on the best information we have, we may trust we'll be better off by taking the particular step.

When I asked Betty out, she did accept; but after a few dates it ended, after I told her of my epiphany on the mountain. You might conclude I would have been better off never to have asked her out in the first place. In fact, though, some huge benefits came from that brief time of dating her, which continue to enrich my life to this day.

For one, Betty shared with me that her sister was a talented vocalist, whom she believed would fit in Sons of Thunder well. We were about to go full-time and needed a new singer, and so we auditioned her, finding her ideal for us. She served us faithfully for the next two years, and contributed greatly to our music and ministry. Today, 38 years later, she continues to be a close friend and musical associate, and sings in a band I direct locally.

In addition, I grew acquainted with Betty's father, who became a close friend and advisor. Then from 1979 to 2009, he served as president of my ministry's board of directors.

Further, my humbling episode with Betty provided me an invaluable real-life lesson about how not to approach talking seriously with a woman. It not only was a priceless learning experience for me personally, but one I've been able to share with countless others, both in teaching and counseling. And so many others have also benefited from my misstep.

The point simply is, don't be afraid to seek God's guidance, and then to open yourself to the unspeakable adventure of following it. Let's say—to note just one of many scenarios that might occur—that on your personal retreat you feel prompted to look up an old friend whom you haven't seen for years. You may find she welcomes you with open arms. Or she may tell you she's attached now and unavailable. If this disappointment occurs, though, you may still learn a vital lesson or two from the experience, which helps you in making other contacts. And then there's the amazing ripple effect that comes from keeping your life in motion. She tells another old friend that you contacted her, and this woman—whom you've long forgotten—is intrigued and contacts you. A relationship develops, and she becomes the one you marry. Such surprise happy endings do happen, and more frequently than you might imagine. But they require that you keeping stepping forward, staying faithful to the light God throws on your path.

And then there's that more mysterious principle of success spoken of in Scripture, akin to casting seeds, which we noted in the chapter on rejection. "Sow your seed in the morning, and at evening let not your hands be idle, for you do not know which will succeed, whether this or that, or whether both will do equally well" (Eccles 11:5-6). As we respond to God's promptings, we'll find that results we welcome sometimes come, and other times not. In hindsight, we realize God had different purposes in these steps we've taken— to stretch and deepen us in one case, but to bless and provide for us in another.

This is why it's so critical to continue to seek fresh guidance, even in the face of disappointment, and to keep striving toward our goal—for in time our persistence is likely to win us the victory we seek, and make our heart's desire possible.

Ten

* * * * * * * * * *

Taking Inventory of Friendships Past and Present

ONCE I DECIDED TO STRAIGHTEN UP A BASEMENT ROOM where I store books, manuscripts and recordings. While about the task, I came across a proposal for a book on conquering shyness that I had drafted about six years before. I had set that proposal aside then, fearing my book idea wasn't compelling enough to interest my publisher. Seeing it on the shelf now drew my interest, though, and made me wonder if I had abandoned that project too quickly. I stopped tidying up, sat down and read through the manuscript—a 20-page condensed version of the book that had been in my mind then.

Now I *liked* what I was reading. In fact, I liked it tremendously, and wondered why I had grown discouraged with the project before. I made a few small changes in the manuscript, and then presented it to the publisher, who welcomed it and commissioned me to write the book. In 1993, *Overcoming Shyness* was published in America, and over the next few years, several international publishers also released it.

Here's what's most striking: At the time I decided to clean up that room, I was eager to find a subject for a new book, and had hit several dead ends. But I had completely forgotten about my previous intrigue with shyness, and this proposal I had labored over before. I pride myself on my memory, and my ability to remember minor details of long-past experiences. Yet this blatant answer to my needs, sown in my past experience and work I had already done, just wasn't coming up on my radar.

By now, I'm sure you know the point I building up to. No matter how sharp your memory, or how brilliant and deep thinking you are, you can hold only so much in your conscious mind at a given time. A perfect solution for a certain need may be there for you, even staring you in the face, but you'll miss it altogether if your focus isn't right. Doing something specific to help your mind fully scan your options makes a huge difference in seeing them clearly. This is as true with relationships and finding someone to marry as with any other need.

Taking inventory in any area where you're eager for new options or ideas, or hoping to find hidden treasure, can yield wonderful surprises. This happened by default for me when I straightened up that basement room. But I could have achieved the same result if I had deliberately reviewed past book ideas, and considered whether any I had shelved was worth considering again.

Using this same process to carefully consider your opposite-sex acquaintances can be enormously helpful in finding a spouse. It may lead you to discover someone to marry among those you know but have overlooked. So let's look now at the practicalities of doing it.

Making It Happen

Taking inventory of your relationships with the opposite sex can yield such stunning insight, that it makes sense to devote some premium time to it. A well-planned personal retreat provides the best possible setting. It's hard to exaggerate the benefits that can come from quiet, reflective time given to finding a solution to any personal need. The benefits that may occur in your search for someone to marry are so extreme that I recommend devoting at least a day to this effort. An afternoon of uncluttered time, though, may suffice, if it's impossible to clear a full day anytime soon, and if you plan and protect the time carefully.

Pick a quiet but inspiring setting for your personal retreat. If your home provides this environment—you live in the country, for instance—it may work to do it there. I only recommend this, though, if you live by yourself, or at least can have the home to yourself while you need it, and if you're certain you can tune out distractions. Turn your phones off, and ignore your e-mail, Facebook, etc.!

Contrast and fresh environment help our inspiration process, though, and traveling does as well. Most of us will do our best reflecting in a vacation-type setting, and one that is especially relaxing for us. If at all possible, go away for your personal retreat, and to a place that by its nature inspires you to meditate and think big.

Whether you take your personal retreat at home or away, try to plan it so that you're focused on your retreat purpose for a full day from the moment you awaken until bedtime.

Begin your retreat time by praying for a few minutes. Ask God to guide your thinking throughout the day, and to enlighten you to any past or present acquaintance who might be a good life companion for you. Ask him to fill you with reasonable hope and optimism as you scan your field of potential candidates. Ask him also to help you think clearly about each one, and to recognize good reasons why each might or might not be a good match for you. Most important, ask him to help you make any shift in perspective toward any of them that might be necessary to see that person's potential as a spouse.

Spend some time also thanking him for his blessings in your past relationships, as well as for the benefits you currently enjoy being single. A thankful spirit about the past and present will best enable you to think positively about your future.

Following this period of focused prayer, do your best to maintain a prayerful, meditative spirit for the rest of the day. Remind yourself continuously that this is a special time when valuable insight may break through, and that God may help you see marriage potential with someone whom you haven't considered before. In that spirit, begin to think carefully over your whole field of opposite-sex acquaintances.

These people fall into roughly three categories:

Past friends with whom you haven't been in contact for some time

Current friends, including old ones with whom you continue to stay in touch

Current acquaintances who aren't yet your friends but may have the potential to be.

While you can obviously start by focusing on any of these groups you wish, I recommend beginning with the first—that is, opposite-sex friends with whom you've lost contact. They are the ones you're most likely to overlook in searching for a mate, and it may take the heightened alertness of a personal retreat to recognize a serious possibility among them.

In considering these past friends (and to say the obvious), rule out any whom you know are now married or in a serious relationship. Of course, you won't know the status of some until you investigate, so stay open about those folks for now. As you focus on the ones who may be unattached, strive especially to identify any who had been an unusually good friend to you. It might be someone whom you dated for a while but then broke up with, perhaps because the chemistry didn't seem strong enough, or someone flashier drew you away. Or it might be someone you never dated, but who still was a uniquely supportive friend who greatly enriched your life.

If you are able to identify such a special friend, resist for now the temptation to stereotype this person as merely a great friend but not a potential spouse. Yes, this is how you thought about that person then. But consider three things:

1. You haven't seen this old friend in some time. She has grown and changed in certain ways, and is a different person now who may deserve another chance. You also have matured; your perspective on the ideal marriage partner has likely changed—hopefully, reading this book has helped reshape it! You may feel instinctively different about this person if you revive your friendship.

Evie and I recently attended one of the most jubilant weddings I can remember. The couple, Robert and Allison, had been great friends in high school and hung out constantly. Robert, though, never wanted a serious relationship with Allison then, because she was "too wild," and Allison considered Robert too serious. They went different ways after high school and lost contact. Then, a year ago, Robert decided to look up Allison again, both of them now in their mid-thirties. The seeds for friendship were still there, and it reignited quickly. But both had matured—Allison is now a respected high school teacher—and each thought differently now about their perfect match. These differences made possible a serious relationship and, soon, the desire to marry.

Theirs is a storybook example of the best possible outcome that can come from taking the risk of looking up an old friend. It doesn't always turn out this way, of course. But sometimes you find the changes that have taken place within you both make your friendship ripe for a wonderful new direction.

2. Consider also that God typically takes us to important places in our lives not through a straight path but a circuitous one. It's at least possible he brought this person into your life initially so you would become friends, but then separate, maybe even for a long period, so that you both would grow in certain ways that would eventually suit you to reunite and marry. If this is true with this friend you're considering, of course, hindsight will eventually be 20-20—so stay open to this possibility for now.

3. The fact that you enjoyed a wonderful friendship with this person before will provide an instant bond and strong basis for reviving it. No matter how old or long-neglected the friendship is, you two have more points of common interest than you probably realize. We each are insatiably intrigued with our own past, and especially with the history we share with someone else. You'll probably find it natural to probe endlessly with this person about what happened to different people, and to places and institutions that defined your life at that time. In the best case, the old friendship provides an exceptional basis for growing a serious relationship, and the deeper, enduring companionship needed for marriage. The benefits that an old friendship can bring to marriage are so extreme, that it makes every sense to begin your search for a partner there, and to consider carefully whether an old friend may indeed be ideally suited to become your partner for life.

Now, with these three thoughts in mind, consider some specifics about this friendship itself, as best as you can remember it, and as best as you can imagine it revived again:

1. Did this friendship have the very best elements? Were you naturally supportive of each other, encouraging to each other, there for each other? Did you laugh a lot together? Was it just plain fun being with this person, and something you always cherished? Did this friendship bring out the best in both of you?

Friendships, of course, come in every flavor. Even the strongest friendship can evolve for all the wrong reasons: you're drawn to each other because you enjoy the same addictive habit, for instance, and stick together to support each other's destructive behavior. If your old friendship tended to bring out the worst in you both, it isn't worth trying to revive it again, unless both of you have changed substantially.

But if it was a healthy friendship, a positive, redemptive force in both your lives, springing from compassion and supportiveness, then you have reason to hope you'll both benefit from reviving it again, and that the basis for something more may now be there.

2. Even if you didn't feel romantically or sexually attracted to this person then, is it at least possible you might feel so now, given how you've changed and grown? Or, if you did feel such attraction then but thought it wasn't strong enough for marriage, might you feel differently now if your friendship revived? Fantasize some about these possibilities, and see what you conclude.

3. Imagine what it might be like to be married to this person. Not just in a serious relationship, but *married*—pulling together in the day-to-day tasks of raising a family (if you choose), building a home, and supporting each other in achieving your dreams. Muse about that possibility for a few minutes, enough to let your feelings settle. How does this fantasy feel? Amazingly good and right in every way? Alien and just not you? Somewhere in-between?

4. Did this person ever indicate she was interested in a more serious relationship with you than you wanted at the time, or even marriage? Or did you sense so, even though he never said it explicitly?

5. Is there any clear and compelling reason why this person absolutely, positively would not be a right match for you? Some possibilities:

> • *You're certain, beyond a shadow of a doubt, that you couldn't feel sexually attracted to this person, regardless of changes that have taken place in your lives since you last saw each other.*
> • *Your preferences and/or lifestyles are too different to mesh well in a lifetime union.*
> • *This person has declared himself/herself to be gay.*
> • *You know that she has developed an addictive habit, or has shown some other major character flaw ruling her out as a marriage possibility.*

- *You know that he is resolved never to marry, or (for some clear reason you know) would never be interested in marrying you.*
- *He or she has an unstable relationship past that makes marrying this person too risky.*
- *You've become a serious Christian since you last saw this person, who is ardently devoted to another faith.* (Don't rule her out just because you're uncertain of her spiritual status; God has been working in his life also, as in yours, and he may also have become a Christian. God may use your influence as well to bring this person to Christ; stay open to that possibility for the moment.)

Now—if you answered yes to questions 1, 2, and 3, and no to question 5, chances are good it will be worthwhile to look up this old friend again. If you also answered yes to question 4, you have a further reason to renew contact, and one that hopefully will boost your confidence about doing so. Keep this person strongly in mind as you continue your personal retreat and consider other people. By the end of the day, you may have identified several old friends to contact, and will want to prioritize these possibilities as best as you can.

Don't be afraid to dig back *really* far into your past, in considering old friends to look up again. I recently ran into a female friend from childhood who, coincidentally, is dating a man I've just recently met. Margie was a neighbor and classmate when my family lived in Fairway Hills, a small community near Bethesda, Maryland. We moved away when I was only ten, and I never saw her again. Yet now after more than fifty years, it was easy to talk with Margie, and natural to pick up our friendship again, and we found much to reflect on from that ancient period of our early childhood.

Even more interesting is the experience of Herb, a childhood friend whom I still see often. In sixth grade, he and I both enjoyed hanging out with a classmate, Evan. That summer, though, her family moved to a different school district about ten miles away. During autumn of seventh grade, Herb and I made several long bike trips to visit her at her new home. We toted along a camera, and shot some photos of her frolicking in the leaves, which we blew up into 8"/10" glossies in my basement darkroom. Our lives moved on after that, though, and we lost contact with her.

Until a few months ago, that is, when Herb decided to look her up again, finding she now lives 3,000 miles away in Seattle. She was thrilled when Herb phoned her, and they chatted a long time. As it turns out, she vividly remembers our seventh grade visits—they were emblazoned in her memory, and she was eager to know if we still had the photos.

And yes, I understand the flip side well. Evan might have been offended that Herb, after fifty-plus years, suddenly phoned her out of the blue. She might have thought him presumptuous, and might even have hung up on him. You take a certain risk when you look up an old friend, and you may be disappointed—even embarrassed. But, honestly now . . . *so what*??? Your old friend isn't going to take out a restraining order on you for one contact. And, in truth, this person's response is much more likely to be exuberant—like Evan's—than the opposite. Nothing ventured, nothing gained. And considering what's at stake, the risk is greatly worth taking. In the best case, your effort will change the direction of both your lives, and bring benefits that last a lifetime.

From Past Friends to Present

Allow yourself at least an hour to muse over your past, in search of a special someone you may have been overlooking. Effective meditation takes time; and with the benefit of such unfettered time, your mind may ante up some surprising possibilities, if not a Eureka moment.

Once you've spent some reasonable time musing over past friendships, move on to focus on present ones. If you've identified one or more old friends to possibly contact, keep them on your A-list for now as you ponder current acquaintances. If no possibility from the past has emerged, don't despair; it may not be God's intention for you to renew contact with an old friend—this is just one possibility to consider. But stay open to any further insight about past friends that may come as the day moves on.

Now give some equal time to inventorying your present opposite-sex friendships. Here's the most important question to consider: Do you currently have such a friendship that you consider *outstanding*? And is it outstanding for each of you? Do you both benefit greatly from each other's encouragement and support? Do you instinctively care for each other and look out for each other? Do you naturally enjoy hanging out together and doing certain fun things together? Are you comfortable confiding in each other, and do you often seek each other's counsel?

Is this person unmarried and unattached at this time?

If you're a Christian, is your friend one also, and is your friendship a positive one spiritually—that is, do you inspire each to grow in Christ?

No friendship is perfect, and you're surely aware of imperfections in this one. But overall, do you regard this person as an exceptional friend? Maybe your best friend of the opposite sex? Possibly even your *best friend*?

If this truly is an exemplary friendship, then, well, you know where this is heading. Can it possibly transform into a serious relationship? And would you be able to see this person from a new standpoint—as someone you could marry? These, of course, are two-way questions, and this part is vital to consider carefully before going further. The risk can be greater—sometimes much so—in raising the question of getting serious with a current friend than with an old, forgotten one. If you draw significant support from this friend, and would be distraught if talk of marriage damaged the friendship in any way, then you should proceed cautiously. If you strongly doubt your friend would respond positively, then you shouldn't broach the topic at all.

On the other hand, you may know quite well that this person would like a more serious relationship with you, or you have good reason to suspect so. Or you may be uncertain, yet you know the friendship is strong enough to endure talk of marriage, regardless of how your friend responds. You can't remove all element of risk—nor the fear of it—when you seek to change the nature of any friendship. But if in all honesty you believe it likely will survive such a serious talk, then the risk is worth taking, given the possible prize.

This current friend, of course, can be someone you're dating, but so far haven't thought of marrying. If this person is an extraordinary friend, though, now is the time to consider if the relationship offers greater possibilities than you've recognized.

Assuming you decide it's worth the risk to broach getting serious with your friend (or getting more serious, if you're already dating), then you're free to consider whether you would be open to marrying this person. And, here again, the personal retreat can provide a ideal context to unwind, let your thoughts flow freely, and consider whether a fundamental shift is possible in how you view this person. Keep in mind that inertia is a tough force to break. If you've lived for some time with the assumption that this person, while an amazing friend, is *just* a friend, and can never be anything more, then this concept will stay in place unless it's strongly challenged. You also have something invested in wanting to be right about this assumption—that is, it may take some swallowing of pride to even consider another possibility.

But, keeping in mind that God is known for great surprises, let everything be on the table for the moment, and let pride take a needed vacation. Muse freely about what it would feel like to be married to this person. Do you feel a surge of peace or "rightness" about it? Even if romance hasn't been central in this relationship before, can you imagine enjoying physical intimacy with this person? Recall what we've stressed before—that moderate physical attraction usually serves a marriage better than extreme, and that strong friendship is the best basis for an enduring, happy physical relationship.

Yes, you may be able to think of others who entice you more physically. But do you feel at least *some* romantic and sexual attraction for this friend? And when combined with the other positive aspects of your friendship, is there a mix of factors that could make for a great marriage? Think about this possibility for a few minutes, and see what your instincts tell you.

There is, of course, no right or wrong answer to this question. You may conclude that even though this person is your best friend on earth, he/she is not someone with whom you want to share life day-in and day-out at the intimate level required for marriage. On the other hand, you may find that in the inspirational setting of the personal retreat, you see this relationship through a different lens. No matter how this person might fall short of your fantasy image of the perfect mate, certain positive aspects of the friendship trump its imperfections. Its unique combination of pluses could segue naturally into a magnificent marriage. You sense this possibility instinctively, and the thought of being married to this person is warmly reassuring.

Now . . . before you yell, *"Eureka, I've found it!"* and start running up and down your hotel's halls, pounding on other guests' doors with the news, remember, this is a day for taking inventory of *all* your opposite-sex friendships. So, do you have another one to consider? Perhaps several? If so, spend equal time musing over each one from the standpoint of its marriage potential. If you conclude that any other naturally has the right qualities for marriage, or could develop them, make a note of this, and take encouragement that, at the end of the day, you'll have more than one option to pursue—if you need it.

Acquaintances

Once you've spent some ample time considering past and present opposite-sex friendships, one more important step remains in the inventorying process. Think carefully now over acquaintances with the other sex whom you don't know well. These may include coworkers, neighbors, classmates, and members of any association, networking group, troupe, club, or social group to which you belong. Of course, someone among these people may set your heart pounding whenever you see her or him—the bombshell who always wears her skirts a few inches too short, or that tall, confident guy whose cologne drives you crazy. But honestly, and realistically, is there someone among this field of associates with whom you naturally feel you could build a special friendship, which could have the right qualities for marriage?

You will have to trust your instincts much more with this group of people than with old and current friends. But that's what a personal retreat is for—to give your instincts the best possible opportunity to guide you reliably. While you may not have much to go on with some of these folks, what do you have? Is there someone among them whom you instinctively like, who usually is friendly to you? Does this person seem by nature to be compassionate, caring, and unselfish? Do you find yourself joking or bantering with him? Does she typically smile at you when you see each other? Is it a *natural* smile she can't help but display, and not forced?

Did I mention, trust your instincts? With this group especially, you don't want to get bogged down looking for too much information, because you just don't have it at this point. These are individuals whom, by definition, you barely know. And, again, don't expect God to provide you more guidance than the light unto your path; he isn't going to reveal that a woman in your swim club whom you've only spoken with briefly is the one you'll marry. But he may prompt you to pursue getting to know her better; that level of guidance is fully reasonable to expect from him. And there's no more likely place for it to happen than a personal retreat.

It's possible no one from this group will emerge as a prospect, and in that case don't force the question. God may or may not have an opportunity for you among them. But take advantage of the inspirational benefits of the personal retreat to explore the possibility. Spend some reasonable time considering these people and the possibility of getting to know any of them better. See if you feel inspired to try to build a significant friendship with any of them. Even if that thought has never struck you before, give credence to it if it occurs in this setting.

Prioritizing

Once you've reflected sufficiently over these opposite-sex acquaintances whom you don't know well, the inventorying process is almost over. I commend you for reaching this point, and you should congratulate yourself as well, for you've already taken a major step toward your goal of finding someone to marry. Even if you haven't been able to identify a single compelling prospect among past and present friends and acquaintances, you've still done two very important things: You've "cleared the deck" with people you know, and can feel comfortable now moving beyond this group to look at steps you can take (and there are many!) to meet someone new.

You've also unleashed your mind, heart, and spirit, and engaged your subconscious mind more fully, in the process of searching for a mate. You may still find that in the days ahead, you suddenly think of someone you've overlooked who's an intriguing possibility. If this happens, you can thank the personal retreat for setting the inspiration process in motion.

If you've come out of the inventorying process with one compelling prospect, then you have an uncomplicated result, at least at this stage. But if you have two or more of them, try to put them in some order of priority. One may obviously interest you more than the others. If not—if they seem equally attractive—then do a bit more reflecting about them. First, pray for five minutes about each one. For each, thank God for bringing this person to your mind, and ask him to help you better understand whether he or she is truly right for you, and the one you should contact first. After praying, spend a few more minutes considering these people—up to an hour if necessary for all of them. Muse comfortably about what it might be like to be married to each one, and pay attention to any stirrings of heart.

Finally, go ahead and simply trust your instincts. Order your prospects in light of how they most interest you at this time. If they still seem evenly weighed, then use a random process to choose between them. If you have two prospects, flip a coin; if three or more, write their names on slips of paper and draw them from a cup. God can guide this random choosing process as well, as he often did casting lots in the Old Testament! But pray for a moment before doing it, asking that, even with your limited understanding, God will make clear to you whom you should pursue first, second, etc.

Finally, close your personal retreat time with a few minutes of prayer, thanking God for his blessings and enlightenment during the day, and asking for his continued guidance as you move forward. If you've identified a current friend or acquaintance with whom you hope to discuss the possibility of marriage, jump ahead to chapters 14-16—on dating and serious talk—where I advise about how to convert a present friendship or acquaintance into something more. If it's an old, forgotten friend with whom you would like to consider marriage, on the other hand, continue reading this chapter for some advice on how to break the ice with this person. (If you haven't been able to identify anyone old or current who interests you, move on to the next chapters, where we'll look at the multitude of steps you can take to meet new prospects.)

Renewing Contact with an Old Friend

While the idea of discussing marriage with a certain old friend may be a wonderful fantasy for the moment, imagining the steps you would have to take to get there may leave you feeling too intimidated to try. The challenge may seem just too overwhelming. Yet keep in mind two things. One is that you don't have to go from A to Z with this person all at once, in fact, you definitely shouldn't try to. Your initial goal shouldn't be to convince this person to marry you, but merely to convert this old friendship back into a current one. In that state, discussing marriage with this person may be totally natural. But you should let your friendship with her resurface and become strong again, before making any effort to talk about getting serious or marrying.

Second is that the explosion of Internet options, including e-mail, Google searches, and social networking sites—Facebook especially—have made reconnecting with old friends vastly easier, and much more permissible, than was true just a few years ago—and far less stressful for you to do as well. If you're a Facebook member, reaching out to old, forgotten friends not only is permissible, but almost a mandate. If you contact a friend whom you haven't seen or spoken with in years, and do it appropriately, chances are very good this person won't view your effort as presumptuous, but as a gracious courtesy. And chances are good you'll get a positive response, providing of course your friendship with him or her was significant in the first place.

If you can't find this person on Facebook, or you're not a member, contacting them by e-mail may work just as well. So much reconnecting goes on by e-mail that your old friend isn't likely to think you're out of place renewing contact this way, again, providing you do it appropriately.

And the great news is that you'll feel much less pressured contacting your old friend initially by e-mail or Facebook than by phoning her. And you'll likely make it easier for her as well. Usually, in fact, I don't recommend contacting an old acquaintance first by phone, unless you're absolutely certain he'll welcome the call. If you're not, then this is a risk you probably shouldn't take. Even if he's glad to hear from you, getting that first contact by phone compels him to interact with you before he may feel ready and has the chance to measure his response. The cold call may simply be too abrupt, and may leave him thinking you're insensitive. Contacting him online is ideal, for it allows him the chance to adjust to your sudden show of interest in him, and to give some thought to his reply before sending it.

You may have to do some sleuthing to find her e-mail address, but you can probably locate it. Consider first whether you know someone who likely knows it, whom you can e-mail or phone about it. You don't need to tell this person why you want to get in touch with this old friend; just saying "I need to contact so-and-so" is enough.

A Google search may reveal his address as well. Remember that he may have a work e-mail as well as a personal one. Include his employer in your search, if you know it.

If you hit a dead end looking for her e-mail address, the next best approach is to send her a brief letter. For this, of course, you need her home address. But that is often easier to locate than an e-mail address. You can search online phone company records for free online, and more advanced searches of public records are available online for a small fee. Another old friend may be able to give you her address as well. If you can't locate a home address, do you know her employer? You can probably find its address online, and if other options fail, it's okay to write her there.

If you're not able to find a mailing address for him, then you'll need to set him aside as a prospect, for the moment at least. You may think of another way to locate him in the near future. Or, because you're now open to it, serendipity may occur—you run into him in public unexpectedly, for instance, or he suddenly pops up on Facebook.

If you do find a mailing address for him, then send him a short letter. Start by noting you've been thinking about him recently, wondering how he's doing, and that you would enjoy renewing contact. Invite him to e-mail you, and provide your e-mail address (plus, of course, your return mailing address, on the chance—though unlikely—he isn't online). Add a couple of paragraphs about your life in recent years. Keep it positive and cordial, but brief. Don't overwhelm him with information, as too much detail may convey neediness on your part and scare him away. Sign the letter "Your old friend, Judy," or some such way, and mail it. Pray for the best and that he'll be moved to e-mail you in response.

If your first contact of this old friend is by e-mail, then compose a similar note for the initial post. Explain that she's come to your mind recently, and you're curious how she is and where life has taken her. Mention that you would enjoy hearing from her and catching up a bit. And include a couple of brief paragraphs about your life's odyssey. Sign it cordially, and press send.

The first e-mail response that comes from this person—if you receive one—will speak volumes about his or her potential interest in renewing friendship with you. If he is married now, he will hopefully tell you. If he is dating someone seriously, he may divulge that also. At the other extreme, she may drop obvious hints that she would enjoy friendly contact with you again. Some positive indications—

- *She specifically mentions she is currently unattached*
- *Her e-mail is chatty, lengthy, highly cordial*
- *She asks specific questions about you*
- *She explicitly says she hopes to hear further from you*
- *He indicates interest in seeing you*
- *He expresses appreciation for your contacting him*
- *He affirms you in other ways*
- *He reminisces about your old friendship.*

If her e-mail includes at least several of these positive indications, it's a good sign she's interested in communicating more with you. Respond with another e-mail of your own. Show interest in the details she provided about her life, and compliment her for anything that deserves affirming (she mentioned a degree she earned, for instance, or a career success). See where it goes, and whether she again responds in kind.

On the other hand, if his first reply is brief, or close to the vest, he may be implying he isn't interested in reviving your friendship. On the chance he may be open to it but simply cautious, you may try e-mailing him one more time. Keep it fairly brief, but thank him for his reply, and affirm him in any way that's appropriate for the detail he provided. Ask him a question or two related to that information, to show interest in him and his life experience. Again, mention that you would enjoy hearing further from him. See if he responds again. If his next reply is more open and chatty, you may have succeeded in breaking through his reserve. If you don't receive another response, or it's as reserved as the first one, then I advise you to drop this person as a prospect.

Again, your goal at this point is to reestablish the old friendship into a new and hopefully thriving one. If e-mailing with this person picks up steam, that's a good indication you're succeeding. You're on good ground after several positive exchanges to state that you would enjoy seeing her, and to ask if it's possible to get together. Posing that question is an acid test of where things really stand, to be sure. If she responds enthusiastically, and you're able to set up a meeting, you have a potential breakthrough. If he turns down your request, ignores it, or is evasive, then it's probably time to let this prospect go, as disappointing as that may be.

Assuming she does agree to meet with you, and you go through with it, you're now in a position to try to move this friendship to a higher level. In that case, go ahead and read chapters 14-16 for advice on initiating dating, courting, and serious discussion about marriage.

And congratulate yourself on a huge accomplishment—for you've succeeded in converting a dormant friendship into a live and vital one once again!

Eleven

* * * * * * * * * *

Starting from Scratch: Putting Yourself in the Right Context

AMONG THE HAPPIEST MEMORIES FROM MY DAYS AS A young single are times when a dating relationship ignited quickly with a woman I had only recently met. I had this joyous experience on four occasions.

In one case, a friend introduced me to a woman he was dating, and I spoke with her just briefly. A month later, upon hearing they had broken up, I asked her out. In another instance, a friend set me up on a blind date with an acquaintance visiting from out of town. I met the third woman at a church bowling social—then asked her out the next day. I met the fourth on a retreat where I led singing; she phoned me the following week and invited me to a movie.

In each of these instances, a dating relationship resulted that boosted my morale enormously. Two of the friendships were so strong that they outlasted the dating relationships and continue to

this day—more than forty years later—even though we've all long
been happily married to others.

These successes occurred not because I possessed some unusual gift for charming women or had earth-shattering sex appeal. I
was a short, skinny guy who failed in some of his most earnest
attempts to win a girl's affection. Yet sometimes I succeeded. My
ultimate success, as I've mentioned, came with a woman I had
known for some time as a friend but hadn't considered more seriously. Yet I had these victories as well, which point to a different
way it works for many of us.

Many who enter a good marriage marry a friend with whom
they enjoy some important personal history. For them, friendship
often precedes romance and any thought of marriage. Yet probably
just as many marry a new acquaintance, with whom they share no
past history. Friendship may precede romance in this case, or romance friendship; often they develop at about an equal pace.

If you've taken inventory of your opposite-sex friendships and
concluded none has the potential to blossom into a serious relationship and marriage, don't despair. God may intend you to marry someone you haven't met yet—as many who happily marry do. I share
these dating experiences of my own because they're so typical of
those seeking love and marriage, and demonstrate how quickly a
new relationship can kindle. If you long to be married, but don't
see any good prospect on the horizon, you still have great reason
for hope. Let's look now at what you can do to spark a new friendship that will lead to marriage.

There are three major ways you can take serious initiative to
find someone to marry whom you haven't met before. They include—

   *1. Putting yourself in the best social settings for meeting this
person*

   *2. Getting help from others, including friends, pastors, and—
possibly—a professional matchmaker*

   3. Making good use of more anonymous approaches, such as

online dating/matchmaking services.

You can, of course, pursue more than one of these options at once, and probably will want to do so. We'll look carefully now at each of these approaches, and I'll try to help you determine what steps will be most productive for you.

Putting Yourself in the Right Context

If you want to meet someone to marry, it's vital to keep two almost paradoxical principles in mind. One is that you need to stay highly active socially, even when your practical side tells you it's futile to take advantage of the opportunities you have. Yes, of course you can overdo it. I'm not suggesting you must fill every waking moment not working with social activity. Each of us needs a certain amount of down time and private time, for our own renewal. But it's critical to be very honest with yourself any time you, say, choose to stay home rather than attend a social event. Do you really need the respite, or are you just caving in to discouragement?

If it's Sunday night, for instance, and you're thinking it's beyond hope that anything good can come from visiting the church's singles meeting yet again, you need to realize this is depression talking and not good judgment. This is where you need to push through the depression and go anyway—assuming this is, to your knowledge, your best opportunity at the moment.

The other principle is that you should research carefully and find the very best opportunities available in your region for meeting someone, and take full advantage of them—even if it means exiting certain situations that aren't working well for you (like the ingrown singles group) . No matter where you live, excellent opportunities exist, providing you're willing to drive a bit. If you've given one situation a fair shake and haven't found it promising, don't hesitate to leave it in favor of another that improves your prospects. Be the best possible steward of your time and opportunities.

Don't underestimate the difference a simple change in venue

can make. And don't make the very common mistake of thinking you already know all the good social opportunities in your area. Chances are strong good options exist that either you haven't discovered or you've judged unfairly. Keep an extraordinarily open mind, and be willing to experiment boldly.

I've already shared how becoming active at Bethesda's Fourth Presbyterian Church when I was almost 20 radically improved my social life, and led to meeting my wife. Here's what's most ironic about that: My parents belonged to a large country club just across the street. I grew up attending that club's functions and spent many summer days camped out at its pool. The club had wonderful activities and was a fertile social climate for many. But, for whatever reasons, it didn't work for me; I never made a single new friend there nor met a single girl to date. I was well aware a large church stood right across the street. But never in my wildest dreams did I imagine it would provide an extraordinary social environment for me. I pictured it as a dead, sterile place socially; I simply didn't have a clue.

There may be a similar opportunity waiting for you to discover where you live—a place where you can thoroughly reinvent your social life, but one that you've long overlooked. Be boldly optimistic and hopeful about finding it, and try every door you can.

In looking for golden opportunities to meet someone, there are two general options to consider carefully. The first is groups and activities geared specifically to singles. The second is clubs and events featuring activities you enjoy and, if possible, geared to a special skill you possess. Let's look in detail at both of these broad possibilities.

Singles Groups and Activities

Churches. In addition to the unspeakable spiritual benefits churches can provide, they are often outstanding places for meeting those of the opposite sex. If you're a Christian, wanting to marry another Christian, it's a no-brainer: a church provides your best prospect for meeting this person, far and away. If you're not a Christian, not sure if you are, or just not interested in spiritual matters, a church may still offer you a good place for meeting someone (and if some spiritual benefit rubs off in the process, I'll be all the happier!).

Here it must be said that churches come in all varieties. My own preference is for those that proclaim a clear message of salvation through Christ, stress the importance of a personal relationship with him, and take a grace-centered approach to the Christian life. The term "evangelical" is often used today to denote this sort of congregation. Evangelical churches are the minority in many regions, to be sure. While most churches give lip service to a relationship with Christ, it's not their central focus, and you hear little or no talk of the importance of being "born again." Yet within almost every denomination, you do find certain churches that are clearly evangelical. From decades of experience speaking, teaching, and performing music in a wide variety of churches, I can also say that evangelical churches typically have the larger and more active singles ministries.

You may find that a different type of church works better for you. But I urge you at least to give the evangelical church a try. You may discover a surprising match, both spiritually and socially.

A good church can potentially provide two exceptional benefits in your search for a mate. If you become active in the congregation at large, and let your need be known, others may take an interest in helping you, and introduce you around. Married folk who've been members of the church and community for some time, may be especially well positioned to know prospective singles you're not otherwise likely to meet. And they may be creative in arranging ways for you to meet them.

Then there are church singles groups *per se*. Most metropolitan areas of any size have at least one church with a dynamic singles ministry, and larger areas often have many. Smaller churches usually don't have enough singles attending to form an active singles ministry, and the smaller groups do sometimes become ingrown.

You'll want to make a judgment call when you visit any one. Are its members outgoing and friendly to you? Of course, not everyone will be. But do at least some take an interest in you and make you feel welcome?

And do a fair number of people in this group seem to have good self-esteem, and seem to be successful and happy with their lives? Like any church mission, a singles ministry is also for the broken, and there will be a mix of people even in the most dynamic, healthy group. But, in balance, does this group appear to be one that draws newcomers? Does it sponsor frequent activities, is it well organized, and is there evidence that visitors often come? Size does matter, and the larger the group, the more likely it is by definition to meet these criteria.

Finding a church with a vibrant singles ministry can take some work. While the Internet can be a starting point, don't depend on it too heavily. Church web sites are often not well-maintained, and even a thriving singles ministry may not have a good Internet presence—that is, one that presents a realistic picture of it.

Churches typically don't communicate well with each other, either. Even the leaders of one church may have little clue about activities at the church just down the street. Just because the pastor of a given parish tells you he doesn't know of any Christian singles groups nearby, doesn't mean they don't exist. He just may not be in that loop enough to know.

To find the best option, you may simply need to dig some and visit around. Start with the larger churches, which, again, are far more likely to have singles groups. Phone the church office. The receptionist at least should know if the church has a singles ministry, and the time and place of its meetings. Then visit and see for yourself. If you remember no other experience of mine, keep in mind what I shared about the church across the street from the country club. Don't trust your instincts about the singles population of a given church—especially a larger church—until you've given it an honest try. At some point, you're likely to be happily surprised.

If you don't quickly discover a church singles group to your liking, don't get discouraged. It may take some trial and error to find the right one, and you may need to visit more than a few. If you don't find a good one within, say, a half-hour's drive from your home, broaden the radius. It's certainly worth driving an hour or more to participate in a singles ministry that truly meets your needs.

Secular singles groups. Metropolitan areas also typically host singles groups that are not church- or religiously-based, but exist to provide singles of any faith an opportunity to make friends and participate in various activities. These events may vary from elaborate adventures like a cruise or a ski trip, to simpler outings like a bowling night, visiting a museum, or venturing to a club to see a band. Such a group may be geared to those of a certain age range, or open to singles of any age. Joining may be as simple as signing up online for the group's e-mail list, then attending events when you're available.

I'll refer to these as "secular" singles groups, for lack of a better term. They often do have good web sites, and are typically easier to locate and investigate online than church groups. A Google search (type in your city/town's name and "singles groups") will likely yield helpful results. And, of course, asking other single friends for recommendations may yield good options as well.

You may find yourself more on your own at such a group's activities than with a church group, where members may be more prone to welcome you and introduce you around. Yet it varies. You're likely to find in any group that certain people instinctively go out of their way to meet you and draw you in. Yet you'll probably need to take some initiative to meet folks as well, and should simply prepare to do so. You will, in fact, do certain others in any singles group a world of good by introducing yourself and making an effort to get to know them. Your kindness will likely pay big dividends, as you find your new friends return the favor by introducing you to others they know, and suddenly the social ball is fully rolling.

154

Special advice. The main feature of some singles events is an athletic activity or competitive game. Usually the purpose isn't to seriously compete or demonstrate exceptional skill, but to have fun and socialize, and the activity is merely a way for that to happen. Still, you may feel uncomfortable going if you aren't highly skilled at the sport or game, or fear you're less talented than others coming. I certainly empathize. Singles events at Fourth Presbyterian often featured sports or recreational activities, like bowling, volleyball, swimming, or canoeing. I *always* felt less competent than others at these functions, and went into many feeling uneasy. I began to discover, though, that my ability simply to have fun, to laugh at my mistakes, and—especially—to encourage others who felt awkward, made these events highly successful social times for me. I made new friends, and on occasion gained the opportunity to date someone.

I mentioned that an important dating relationship for me began with a woman I met at a church bowling social. She was on my team that evening. Neither she nor I were very good bowlers. But we spent the evening laughing at our blunders, and gently teasing each other. Had I been greatly skilled at bowling, in fact, the dynamics of that evening might have been different, and the relationship might never have ignited.

Which brings me to another vital point: your lack of mastery of a given sport rules out the possibility you'll come across as a showoff. An Olympic-level bowling skill will endear you to your teammates if you're in a league. But it may work against you at a singles social; in fact, you may want to "dumb down" your skill there. We don't win friends by outshining them or trying to impress them, but by supporting and encouraging them. The less-skilled bowler may be better poised—and not too preoccupied—to be a good friend to others attending, and this supportive spirit is what will most impress the opposite sex.

In general, too, people are drawn to us more by our weaknesses than our strengths—*providing* we accept our limitations with grace and good humor—for others want to feel we're on their level and not towering above them. Take encouragement from that, and if you feel awkward going to a certain activity, swallow hard if you have to, but go anyway. By all means, don't shy away because of insecurity about your skill. You'll likely be glad you risked embarrassment and went. And you may find that the very event you most dread is the one where your greatest breakthrough occurs.

Clubs and Associations

On the other hand, it also makes great sense to join a club or association that caters to those with a particular skill or interest of yours, or that supports those in your line of work, or that requires a certain talent you have for its function (an athletic team or an orchestra, for instance). There are numerous types of organizations where your skill is a social benefit, for you're able to contribute to the group's purpose and support others by using it. In this case, making the best use of your talent enriches your social life, and it's far less likely you'll come off as a showoff simply by doing your best.

Such organizations, of course, typically include both single and married members. But even when married outnumber single, that can be an advantage if even a single married person or couple takes an active interest in helping you meet someone. If you simply make it your intent to be a faithful, friendly, and supportive member of the organization, you may be surprised at the social opportunities that open up. For example, a friend of mine has recently seen a wonderful relationship develop with a woman he got to know while attending meetings of his local Junior Chamber of Commerce.

Professional associations, in fact, are a good place to begin in looking for organizations that can boost your social life. Carefully research the ones in your community. Note any that cater specifically to those in your line of work, as well as those that support all professionals or workers in your area. Include both conventional organizations like chambers of commerce, Lions Club, Kiwanis, etc., as well as more contemporary, less formal "networking associations." If you can only attend one, try to identify which provides the best opportunity for meeting singles of the opposite sex. If there's no easy way to determine this, then pick the organization whose meetings are best attended. Choose the one that seems your best option, then become an active, supportive member. You will certainly expand your social life and benefit in many ways professionally. And you may just meet the love of your life.

Beyond professional associations, there are countless groups and organizations catering to enthusiasts of a particular skill, topic, or activity. Which reminds me of the story of a young man who bragged to a friend that in his spare time he hunted bear with a club. When his astonished friend asked how he possibly did it, the young man confessed, "Well . . . there are 25 of us in the club." There are indeed clubs that hunt bear, and just about any other creature you can imagine.

It's a good idea to take inventory of your personal interests and skills. Is there an activity you greatly enjoy? Or a skill you long to develop? Or a talent at which you already shine? Take heart that this interest or skill may be the entree to a richer social life for you, for there's quite possibly an association or club near you that caters to it.

And don't be too quick to think a certain skill or interest of yours is too obscure or irrelevant to help your social life. Let's say you play flugelhorn. And you not only played it in high school and college orchestras, but actually *enjoy* playing the instrument. And you would love the chance to perform again and hone your skill. But you're thinking the flugelhorn doesn't have the sex appeal of the guitar, drums, sax, or other rock instruments, and it isn't likely to make you a standout with the opposite sex. But hold on. A community orchestra probably exists within 30-60 minutes of where you live. They pop up in unusual places, and you find them in both rural and metropolitan areas. And in the community orchestra you have a large group of people who, like yourself, enjoy playing a "non-sexy" instrument and love out-of-the-mainstream instruments.

And if you're able to contribute positively to this organization, you'll be a star.

And you may just find that the cute oboe player several chairs over, recently widowed, is drawn to you and a wonderful relationship develops. Or, at a performance, a woman in the audience who plays flugelhorn approaches you afterward because she shares your love for the instrument—and that conversation sparks an ongoing friendship that leads to marriage. It happens, my friend, and it happens exactly like this to those who put their life in motion at the point of a creative gift.

And it happens to those who, regardless of their skill, are participating with others in an activity they love: traveling with the ski club, bowling with the Friday night league, chatting about a recent release with the book club, working out with the gym's aerobics class, pondering the next move with the investment club, discussing spiritual matters with the Bible study, practicing with the church choir, volunteering with a dedicated group at the shelter or food bank. Not to mention the educational alternative: taking a class at a local college or through your county's continuing education—not only to study an interesting topic, but for the social benefit.

I recall the fortunate experience of my father-in-law Glenn Kirkland. Though his vocal talents were, well, limited, he faithfully participated in his church's large choir for years. This commitment rewarded him handsomely in 1991, when, several months after his first wife Grace died, a new member joined named Barbara Neilson. She had endured a difficult divorce, but was eager to marry again—as was Glenn. They simply hit it off. They began dating, then married nine months later. Theirs was a blessed marriage, lasting seventeen years, until Glenn's death in 2008 at 89. This all came about because they both chose to stay active after major disappointments. Had they chosen instead to sit home and wallow in their grief, they would have likely stayed single into their elderly years.

No matter where you live, there are social opportunities available, including some great ones you probably haven't discovered—and very possibly one that can lead to meeting your lifemate. Earnestly research the options available to you, and take advantage of the best ones you can find.

Major Moves

In weighing steps you can take to meet the opposite sex, don't discount the possibly of picking up and moving somewhere else. Metropolitan areas offer broader options for meeting singles than rural—to say the obvious. And some cities have larger singles populations than others, and some a greater percentage of male or female singles. If you truly believe the options for meeting people where you live are too limited, or that you're stigmatized there as a perpetual single, it can make great sense to move to an area that better maximizes your potential for finding a mate. It makes sense, *providing* you go determined to search out and harvest the best opportunities there, and committed to the whole process of making new friends.

Such a move not only can open up a new social life, but affects your psyche positively as well. A major fresh start like this helps renew your hope of finding someone, heightening your alertness to opportunities, and energizing you to be proactive.

Some Christians who would love to make such a move feel uncomfortable, fearing they would be pushing God's hand. "If God wants me marry," they ask, "can't I assume he'll make it happen where I live now? Wouldn't moving be taking matters into my own hands too much, and showing I don't truly believe God will provide for me?"

Here I need to remind you of what we've said before. While God wants you to trust fully that he'll bring the right person along in his own way and time, he also wants you to take proper initiative to find this person—just as you would to advance your career, for instance. It's just as justified to move somewhere else to improve your marriage prospects as to find a better job, and just as likely

God may want you to do so. It's all part of being a good steward of your life and opportunities. And, again, we often demonstrate stronger faith in Christ by taking difficult initiative than by sitting still, for we assume greater challenges that force us to depend on him more fully.

Of course, being a good steward of your life means weighing the big move against other responsibilities you have and what's best for your career. You'll need to consider a number of factors, and the moving decision can be complex. On the negative side, you may be leaving supportive friends who are looking out for you and have good potential to help you find someone (more on that in the next chapter). Yet there often are win-win factors in the big move. It improves your prospects for finding someone to marry *and* allows you to take a better job. And friends who are looking out for you in the rural community where you now live continue to do so after you move to the city. If you don't have such a supportive network now, though, you may be better positioned to develop it in your new locale. Approach the question of moving with bold optimism, and see what new vision develops for your life! You may find moving holds the key to finding your mate.

Summary
The message of this chapter has been simple, yet extraordinarily important: You have the potential of taking steps with your social life that can improve your chances of finding someone to marry, even considerably. While a major geographical move can help greatly, less spectacular changes where you now live—switching to a new church or singles group, joining a club or association—can make a significant difference. And giving each situation a fair chance, and fighting through futility to faithfully attend a group's activities, can yield a sudden, stunning breakthrough as well. The bottom line is, keep your social life active, and as *creatively* active as you can, until your effort yields that prize you're seeking—a special friend to marry.

Twelve

* * * * * * * * * *

Starting from Scratch: Getting Help from Others

THINK ABOUT THE MARRIED COUPLES WHOM YOU KNOW well enough to know how they met. I'll bet the majority were introduced to each other by someone else. Am I right? Take a moment and think over these people, and consider whether this is true. It certainly is for the multitude of couples I've known personally.

Whatever the percentages, many, many couples who marry meet initially because someone is kind enough to introduce them to each other. Sometimes it's simply a courtesy or formality: John introduces his friend Ralph to his cousin Sandy because they're both standing by the punch bowl at a wedding reception. Yet such introductions often are intentional, by one friend or family member wanting to help another find a relationship. They may occur spontaneously, when the chance arises in public, or at a party or event.

Yet often they are carefully planned. Herb invites his new

officemate Sally to dinner at his home, for the express purpose of introducing her to Mac, his best buddy from high school. Or he arranges a blind date for them. Or he encourages them to contact each other, and gives them enough reason to do so.

A friend with this heart and incentive to help you find someone to date or marry is truly the greatest gift imaginable in your search for a mate. If you already have one or more such friends or relatives who are proactively trying to help you, count yourself extremely fortunate. If not, you can do plenty to increase the chance that others will become your allies in your marriage quest.

You don't want to carry your heart on your sleeve nor come off as excessively needy, to be sure. And you certainly don't want to be a pest. Yet neither do you want to be so pride-bound that you never mention your wish to be married to your friends. You probably will need to swallow some pride here. Making a point at least once in a while to tell your friends that you continue to hope to marry and are open to any suggestions, is a good idea.

While of course it's possible an unmarried friend will introduce you to the love of your life, it's more likely a married friend will do it. Your single friends still have to fend for themselves, while your married friends are more emotionally free to think about others' social needs—at least this is often the case. In addition, certain compassionate people who find marriage a great blessing feel a sense of mission to help others find their way to this estate. All of this is why being active socially with married friends as well as single is so important if you want to find someone to marry. Your married friends need the reminder that you're there, eager to marry and available. While spending time with a married friend and taking an interest in his needs may seem irrelevant to your search for a mate, he may be the very person who suddenly, unexpectedly, goes out of his way to introduce you to your match.

There is also a place—a very definite one—for being more assertive about seeking your friends' help in finding someone to marry. Keep in mind that certain people enjoy being helpful, are flattered when you ask their assistance, and may be well-positioned to help you. Pick a friend who is socially active and popular, but also compassionate, and whom you suspect will be happy both to help and advise you. Invite this person to lunch or dinner—your treat!—and tell them it's to seek their advice and possible help on a matter. And, indeed, go into this meeting with two major goals: to get your friend's counsel on how you might improve your chances of finding someone to marry, and to enlist him or her as your ally.

Before you meet, do whatever you can to stoke your desire for your friend's advice. Receiving it may seem the less exciting part of the meeting for you; indeed, it may not seem so at all. But it will likely be the most enjoyable part for your friend, for most people love giving advice. In truth, it may be the most beneficial part for you. Each of us has blind spots that others see well, and we may be doing certain things that, unknown to us, are sabotaging our goal. If you have chronic bad breath or some habit that turns others off, count yourself incredibly fortunate if a friend points this out to you. Correcting the problem may greatly improve your success with the opposite sex. So go eager for your friend's advice. But if eagerness is too hard to achieve, at least be ready to swallow hard and accept any counsel that might sting a little at first but still be helpful to hear.

When you do meet, be sure to thank your friend for taking the time. And tell him he is someone whose insight you strongly respect. Explain to him that you long to be married, but so far have hit roadblocks in your effort to find someone. Does he see anything you might change about yourself or your approach that could make a difference? And does he recommend any steps you might take to meet someone? Give your friend the freedom to pontificate as much or as little as he wants on these points, and accept his advice graciously and non-defensively. Not a bad idea to take along pen and paper and take notes; this will be flattering to your friend, and helpful to you when you're trying to recall his most salient points.

Once your friend seems done offering advice, ask her if she has any more to give. If not, then thank her sincerely for her counsel, and tell her you intend to take it seriously.

It's quite possible that by now she has on her own offered to help you in your search. But if not, make a point now to tell her you would greatly appreciate her keeping an eye out for you. Explain that you're open to meeting anyone or contacting anyone she believes might be a good prospect, and that you're certainly open to blind dates. Assure her you don't expect her to move mountains, but would simply be grateful for any help that's natural for her to provide.

Chances are very strong your friend will respond positively and not leave you embarrassed for asking his help. He may even think of someone on the spot to introduce to you. At the least, you've now set a positive force in motion; your friend will incline more to look out for you now, and may encourage others to do so as well. Compassion, hopefully, will move him to help you, and so will his desire to be helpful and important (most people find it thrilling to know they've introduced another to their match). You've also gained the freedom to remind your friend from time to time that you're still open to his suggestions.

More generally, you've broken the ice now in this task of asking for help, which means you'll find it easier to do with anyone else!

And why not try someone else? If you have several supportive friends, approach them each this way. Invite them to a meal for a tête-à-tête about your desire to marry. Enlist as many as you can in your support network. Don't get too bogged down over whether a given friend who promises to help will actually come through. You just don't know, and you may be surprised. Remember, you don't need 300 leads from these people; you only need one *right* lead. And that may come from the least likely of your friends.

Consider approaching anyone else you know who, even though not a close friend, is in a support relationship with you and compassionate. This could include a pastor on your church staff, an elder, Bible study leader, or Sunday school teacher. It might include also the director of a club or organization to which you belong, or a physician or dentist whom you've come to trust —just as some for-instances. Trust your instincts. If someone among these folks has been kind to you, and naturally likes being helpful, throw caution to the winds and approach them. As always, nothing ventured, noth-ing gained.

Professional Matchmaking

We've been speaking of the informal but very significant role that friends and others can provide you in finding someone to marry. But what about getting help from someone whose *profession* is help-ing others find a marriage partner? Professional matchmakers con-tinue to function widely in many societies today. While not a highly visible presence in America, they do exist here, and do help many find their way to a good marriage. So, should you consider hiring one? *Possibly*. Let's look at the pros and cons, and at whether the tradeoffs are worth it in your case.

Parents, of course, have played matchmaker for their children in countless societies throughout history. While that tradition con-tinues in some cultures, it largely faded in America by the late 1700s, and today is practiced only occasionally by certain religious groups. Unless you happen to belong to a church or religious community where parental matchmaking is encouraged and supported, your parents don't likely have the social connections or know-how to arrange a good marriage for you. While they may help you meet people, and may offer invaluable counsel, it's doubtful you can sim-ply turn over the work of matchmaking to them.

Professional matchmaking offers a different possibility. Historically, clergy and other specially-gifted individuals assisted both independent adults and parents wanting to arrange marriages for their children—often helping men and women of distant towns with no other means of discovering each other to meet and marry. Wherever they exist today, matchmakers still provide this level of service, helping unlikely people connect and marry. In *Getting*

Serious About Getting Married, Debbie Maken provides a moving account of how a matchmaker introduced her to the man she happily married, who then lived a continent away.[15]

While it cannot be said that professional matchmaking flourishes in America today, it does exist, and most of us are at least vaguely aware of that. We've seen the occasional ad, or heard the occasional story about someone meeting their spouse through a matchmaking professional. And they can be found in every major city in our country. It's not unusual to pay several thousand dollars for the services of a competent matchmaker with a proven track record.

Truly skilled matchmakers who view their work as a vital mission can provide invaluable help to those at their wits end searching for a mate, and from time to time I've recommended their services to others. They may be the answer for the excessively shy man who has much to bring to the table as a husband and father, but is traumatized at breaking the ice with a woman. Or for the overwhelmed professional whose career responsibilities leave her little time to socialize. Or for the rural resident with few options for meeting people, but whose work or family responsibilities prevent him from moving to a more socially active area.

Or for one, like Debbie Maken, living away from her home country (India), but wishing to marry someone from there. It was this concern precisely that moved Abraham, in the Bible's most celebrated matchmaking story, to send his servant away from Canaan to his hometown Haran, to look for a wife for Isaac there.

Yet the simple reality is that most in America today who find a good marriage do so without a matchmaker's help. Which is to say, the chances are good you don't *need* the services of this person in your quest for a mate. There is always the danger that, by elevating your search to this level, it becomes too grandiose. As we've stressed, your very best match may be with someone you already know, someone among your longtime circle of friends and associates—someone who shares your history. The matchmaker will likely look beyond your own backyard to places beyond. That may be good if you've truly exhausted your options—but often this isn't the case.

Another problem is that finding a good matchmaker can be challenging. Yes, you can find them through the phone directory and the occasional ad. But it's vital that you're comfortable with the matchmaker you hire, confident she is competent, has wide contacts, and your very best interests at heart. And it's difficult to know all this without solid references—but how do you go about getting them?

Consider that if you move to a new town and ask, say, a half-dozen neighbors or coworker about local services, from that small pool you'll almost certainly glean abundant recommendations for doctors, dentists, auto mechanics, home repair specialists, lawn professionals, restaurants, and places to shop for almost anything. Yet chances are not one of them knows a matchmaker to recommend nor anyone else who does. It's just as unlikely anyone among your longtime friends and associates can recommend one either.

So in looking for a matchmaker, you're in a different territory than in searching for most professional services. Which brings out how critical it is to ask a matchmaker for references, especially of those who are happily married because she connected them. Talk to these people, and make certain they're not just reference plants. Be confident the matchmaker has truly helped them, before entrusting your future—and probably a small fortune—to him.

Speaking of that fee, matchmakers are certainly worth their hire if they introduce you to the love of your life. Spending, say, $3,000 for a quantum leap toward this introduction is a drop in the bucket compared to the lifetime benefits you'll gain. And you may well save more than this from not having to date around. You'll save time to be sure—*if* the matchmaker succeeds. But, of course, there's no guarantee. Unless his fee is contingent on his success, you risk losing your investment. And if you decide to sit in suspended animation till the matchmaker comes through, you may lose time as well, which you could otherwise invest in a more direct effort to find someone.

Having noted these cautions, hiring a matchmaker may be worth the risk, if you can afford it and are convinced your other options are limited. Again, though, your options may not be as poor as you think. Are you certain you've exhausted possibilities among past and current friends? I urge you at least to go through the inventory-ing process I've recommended, to allow yourself the best possible chance to determine if you've overlooked someone. And, again, are there certain changes you can make in your social life that could open up new options, maybe significantly? If so, you might want to make them first and give them a reasonable chance, before engag-ing a professional. Online services offer another major approach to consider, which we'll look at in the next chapter.

But if you simply want to "cut to the chase" in finding a mate, of course it's fine to hire a matchmaker. While cutting to the chase is still what it's all about, the matchmaking process today differs substantially from what it was historically. In the past, those who entered marriages arranged by parents or professionals usually didn't know each other well when they married. Most did have *some* say about the union. But the opinions of parents, family member, and others in the community (who typically stood to benefit economi-cally and sometimes politically from the couple's union), carried major sway. Apart from a compelling reason not to, most accepted the recommendation of their parents or the matchmaker. This is because the expectations of romantic nirvana that fuel the mating process today simply weren't present in any society until about 200 years ago. People viewed marriage primarily as a step toward so-cial and economic security. While the hope of romantic love's blos-soming was usually there, it was accepted as a fringe benefit and not the driving force to marry.

Expectations of intimacy and romantic happiness in marriage are vastly higher today, to say the least. You're far less likely to take a matchmaker's word that she has found your ideal mate than if you had lived, say, in England in the 17th century. I also hope that if this book has done nothing else for you, it has persuaded you that friendship should be the overriding factor moving you to marry someone. And you're not likely to determine if the seeds of a strong, lifetime friendship are there with just a date or two. You'll need to spend more time getting to know a matchmaker's recommendation than people would in centuries past.

Still, if you're confident in a matchmaker's gift for making good unions, you'll view someone he recommends with strong hope you've found your match, and your relationship will launch from this position of strength. You'll likely put the burden of proof on why you shouldn't marry this person, rather than why you should. You'll also have the treasured benefit of knowing this person is serious about considering marriage with you. You'll be able to skip a lot of preliminaries as you get acquainted, in other words, and probably move much more quickly to a marriage decision than otherwise.

While online services often claim to offer matchmaking, they do not provide the special benefits of a real person working for you. Internet dating sites can help you meet people, unquestionably, and many good marriages come from connections made through them. Yet you're largely on your own as you pursue your contacts. No one is there to coach you and hold your hand. You have to do the serious vetting of any prospect yourself, and getting acquainted can be lengthy.

You begin from a greater position of strength with a matchmaker, and in the best case, take a giant step forward in finding your right partner. It's this potential for the quantum leap that puts professional matchmaking in a special category, and makes it worth considering if other efforts seem to have failed. Just keep in mind that your goal should be the same with the matchmaker as with any other approach you take: to find someone to marry with whom your bond of friendship is unusually strong. With God's help, this can happen through a matchmaker's service as successfully as through any other means.

Thirteen

* * * * * * * * * *

Starting from Scratch: Internet Options

THE STEPS WE'VE SUGGESTED SO FAR FOR FINDING A mate are similar in that you seek to build a relationship with someone you've already met in person. You either do so with an acquaintance you already have, or you meet someone in person for the first time and start from there. Options remain, though, where before ever meeting someone in the flesh, you communicate for some time more anonymously. You may even build your relationship significantly before finally meeting in person.

In ages past, it wasn't uncommon for couples to get acquainted first through letter writing. A man and woman might be introduced long distance by family or friends, and then exchange many letters before finally meeting. Today, e-mailing has largely replaced letter writing for this purpose, though a couple might progress to phone chatting for a while before their first "face to face."

If you do start communicating with someone you haven't met because a friend or family member introduces you, you begin your relationship from a wonderful position of strength. The fact that someone you trust has recommended you predisposes you both to positive impressions of each other. Plus, you have the recommender as an ongoing source of information about each other. So you're actually getting acquainted not just through e-mail and phoning, say, but through input from the one who introduced you as well. When you finally do meet face to face, you'll likely be well prepared and not greatly surprised by what you find.

It's a very different world with non-face-to-face options you initiate yourself, such as personals or online dating. Here you're on your own from the start, with no one to advise you about the person you contact. While some continue to use newspaper personals, Internet dating services are vastly more popular today for meeting prospective strangers, and they greatly increase the chance you'll meet someone right for you. I strongly recommend that, if you want to take a non-face-to-face approach to finding someone to marry, choose an Internet service over personals or phone-chat lines. Just be sure to go into the process with your eyes wide open.

With an Internet dating service, you meet someone cold for the first time online. And for a while, your sole information about her comes from her postings online, e-mailing her, and online searches. You may progress to phone chatting. Still, you're largely limited to the information he chooses to divulge before meeting him face to face. When you finally do meet, you both may be in for huge surprises.

I don't say this to bias you against the Internet alternative. Online matching services provide an intriguing option to add to your arsenal of tactics for meeting your mate, and they may work well for you. The online approach does provide certain advantages in your search for the right person:

1. The most obvious is that you enjoy vastly more prospects than ever possible through any other approach. You can consider someone in a distant city or country, and communicate seriously with her before ever traveling to meet her. Even within your own region, you'll find a large number of potential candidates whom you would never otherwise likely meet.

2. *Getting acquainted online rather than in person can be less awkward initially, especially if you find that your new acquaintance isn't right for you.* You don't have to progress to a face-to-face meeting unless you're fully comfortable, and if not, you can "close" this person easily and move on.

3. *You can focus more fully on your ideals.* In the normal, real-life process of searching for someone to marry, you're beginning with specific people you've met in the flesh. You have this person, who meets your ideals in certain ways but not others—this is your starting point. With an online service, you can start with your expectations to a greater extent, and then look for individuals who fulfill them. While you're always limited to the information someone provides in determining how well they match your ideals, you can be more blatantly honest about it, and avoid losing time interacting with those who clearly don't meet your most important expectations.

4. *You can pursue your search on your own time, when you have the time, at the spur of the moment, at the most unlikely times.* If it's 3:00 a.m. and you can't sleep, that's as good a time as any to check out things online. This extreme flexibility of online connecting is especially appealing to busy professionals who find it hard to fit in normal-hour social events where they might make new contacts. Yet it's appealing as well to socially active people who welcome the chance to also do something productive during their idle time toward finding a mate.

5. *The online approach is time-friendly in another way, in that it requires less time than in-person socializing often does.* You don't have to bother with your appearance; no need to take time to fix your hair and dress attractively. And there's no lost time traveling to some event. Just pull up a chair in front of your computer, switch it on, and you're ready to go.

6. *For the excessively shy or introverted person, who is instinctively nervous at social events and panics at the thought of*

introducing himself to someone new, the online approach can be a godsend. It poses much less trauma in the early stage of meeting and getting acquainted, and can allow him a fair chance to warm up in communicating, to the point that he's comfortable meeting an online friend face to face. Often, too, the introvert, with less distraction from a busy social life, has given more attention than the extrovert to developing writing skills. Beginning a relationship online thus puts her in a position of strength, because she naturally communicates well through e-mail.

Drawbacks of Online Matching

While the Internet approach can provide you these special benefits, it also has two major drawbacks that many at first do not appreciate.

One is that it tends to encourage unrealistic expectations—both on your part and that of the person you meet and communicate with online. This often leads to a letdown for both of you when you finally meet in person, and discover that this person whom you've only known through the Internet is, in fact, a flesh-and-blood . . . *human being.*

When a friendship develops naturally with someone you've met in person, you see her from the start "warts and all," as someone with certain wonderful qualities but some rough edges as well. Yet you're willing to accept her less redeeming traits, because her virtues outweigh them. Your nurturing side naturally kicks in also: you feel compassion for him, and want to help him with his problems, and to compensate for those points where he's high maintenance. All of this in the name of maintaining a strong relationship, where reciprocity rules and your friend extends the same benefits to you.

While real-life friendships focus you from the start on specific people, for whom you make many adjustments in your ideals, the Internet process focuses you more on *criteria.* Your primary concern is to find someone who perfectly fulfills all your ideals for the quintessential mate, and so you're less likely to be patient with someone's shortcomings. And whomever you communicate with online likely is similarly minded. The advertising of online services too often fosters this mentality. One television ad for a popular service features a woman proclaiming, "I typed in my recipe for the perfect husband—and I found him!" The men and women featured in both TV and print ads for these sites almost always are beautiful, Hollywood specimens, fueling your fantasy that you can find someone who meets your wildest dreams about physical appearance.

It's also relatively easy during the e-mailing stage to convince each other that you do match one another's fantasies. You naturally swap your most attractive photos, and do whatever possible to present your best side and keep any skeletons in the closet there. The result is a strong chance for disappointment when you finally meet in person. As long as you only communicate online, you are largely fantasy persons to each other. And, unfortunately, fantasy always trumps reality. Far too many, upon finding their fantasies dashed at the first face to face, cut off further contact with their online acquaintance. They never allow themselves the opportunity to get to know this person meaningfully, nor the other the chance to prove herself.

At the other extreme, online communicating can cause you to focus way too much on certain negatives you discover about the other through e-mailing or Internet searching—features you might overlook or even view positively if you knew this person well. The fact that a longtime friend, for instance, holds different political views than you may simply be a footnote to your friendship, and not something that substantially defines it. It may even be a positive factor, stimulating your conversation. Yet in online sharing, such a difference may take on far more importance than it deserves, becoming a glaring negative that colors your whole view of this person. And, sadly, you may never move beyond it to get to know this individual well, and to appreciate his much broader, rich mix of qualities. You see her as an issue, not a person.

You may also be too quick to conclude that certain problems an online acquaintance discloses, or certain needs she details, make her too high maintenance. Yet if a real-life friend had these same problems or needs, they might bring out your nurturing side and give you a welcome sense of being helpful to this person—especially if he also brings important benefits to your life. In this case, you see his issues in the context of a wonderful friendship, whereas they can become the whole basis for judging the relationship with someone you meet online.

This isn't to say that some people aren't highly successful with online dating. Yet my observation is that they're most often the same ones who already enjoy plenty of success with the opposite sex in real life and are skilled at getting dates. The Internet approach simply becomes another means for them to succeed. They're most often the 9s and 10s on those scales of human attractiveness and success, and thus are less likely to disappoint the fantasies of someone they've met online when they finally meet in person.

But what about the woman who, say, is a 5 on these (frankly horrid) scales? She has a huge number of positive qualities to bring to a relationship, and even more to contribute to a marriage than many "9s" and "10s." But her online companion, who has been hoping for someone who looks more like Mariah Carey, is disappointed when they meet in person. He cuts off further contact, and never gives her a fair chance. Were she to develop a friendship with an office mate, on the other hand, or a member of her church, she would be on better ground from the start—for that man wouldn't be entertaining unrealistic fantasies about her, and she would have a more reasonable chance to grow on him.

Making the Online Approach Work

Still, there's hope for her succeeding with online dating, and hope for the vast majority of us who consider ourselves average by any standards of attractiveness and success. Four steps will significantly increase your chance of success with the online approach, and will help you avoid the pitfalls I've just mentioned.

1. Keep in mind from the start that online matching tends by its nature to fuel unreasonable expectations, and determine to do whatever you can to counteract this. Remember that your greatest joy in marriage will come not only from your spouse's meeting certain needs of yours, but also from the pleasure of caring for her and meeting her needs. And remember that God gives us marriage about equally for our fulfillment and for our growth. The Internet will incline you to focus too much on fulfillment and too little on growth—but don't let it. Try your very best to see anyone you communicate with online as a unique human being, and not just someone who meets or doesn't meet certain criteria. Stoke your nurturing side and your compassion. Strive to care for this person whom you haven't yet met face to face, and make one of your criteria the fact that you're able to feel such concern for someone you've only met online.

This sort of attitude will increase the chance you'll choose someone from the start who is a good match for you, and diminish the possibility either of you will be seriously disappointed when you finally meet.

2. At the same time, remember that getting acquainted online can incline you to magnify the other's imperfections—or what you perceive to be such. If he has certain redeeming features you like but falls short at some other points, be certain you're not attaching more importance to these negatives than they deserve. Would you be more forgiving of them if he were a real-life friend you had known for some time and esteemed? If so, it may be well worth meeting him in person and giving the human factor a meaningful chance.

Let's say, for instance, that your Internet companion is a single mom with a five-year-old son. You've always imagined you would want to be married for several years before having children. And so, while you like everything else about her so far, the fact she's already a parent is an overwhelming negative and close to a deal killer. You view the whole relationship and its possibilities through this one filter. Yet if she were a friend you already knew, and you got along well with her boy, would you possibly feel different? And is this possibly an area where God wants to grow and stretch you? Is there a chance that parenting a young child at this time in your life might be good for you, and make you a deeper, more caring person?

Remember, too, that we often are not good judges of what really will make us happy. Can you remember instances when this has proven true for you? You expected to be miserable in certain situations, for instance, but instead enjoyed them immensely? If so, it may be worth giving this woman—and her son—a chance. At least allow this Internet friend the same flexibility you would someone in real life.

3. A third important strategy with online matching is to move to a face to face as soon as possible. Once you actually meet this person, the dynamics change and improve radically—for now you see him as a human being, and not just some abstraction who fulfills or doesn't certain items on your checklist. You owe it both to him and yourself to bring this meeting about as quickly as possible. So, if you like what you're discovering about him after several exchanges online, suggest that you meet for coffee to get better acquainted. If he hedges, you may want to close him and move on to someone else. Remember, you're looking not just for someone to communicate with, but *to marry*—and one of the likely indications he wants to be married is his eagerness to meet in person.

4. Finally, there's a further step I highly recommend that can substantially improve your potential for success with someone you meet online: Look for someone who enjoys an activity you also enjoy, and one you can quickly begin doing together, if you click well enough at your first meeting. If you find in early e-mailing that you don't have such a shared interest, close this person and look for someone else—for the potential of your relationship aborting at the first in-person meeting is simply too strong.

Here's why: If you look at your real-life friendships, you'll find that most, if not all, have developed with people with whom you've done things together regularly. Pick a friend at random; it's probably a coworker, a fellow church member, a student at your school or college, or a fellow member of a team, orchestra, or organization to which you belong. Your shared activity has brought you together frequently enough for your friendship to blossom. It has also given you common experience to talk about (something other than just your relationship!), and this too has done much to spark your friendship.

This is why you're disadvantaged with a friendship that develops online. All you have initially to grow this delicate relationship is communication and the process of getting acquainted at this distance. Unless you both feel an unusually strong spark when you finally meet, the momentum to continue meeting probably won't be there. Yet romantic chemistry can take a while to develop. If there's an activity you can take on together, that's fun and gives you something else to talk about than each other, then you can grow acquainted at a more reasonable pace. And you'll give romance a more realistic chance.

The important thing is having an activity you actually *do* together, and a strong enough common interest that you don't feel awkward suggesting it. You're likely to share certain points of interest with anyone you meet online. You may both enjoy David Letterman, read the same novelist, or feel passionate about the same social cause. But do these interests translate into an activity you can quickly take on together once you start getting acquainted in person?

You can, of course, suggest doing something socially that most people would enjoy, like attending a movie or concert. Yet this smacks of asking for a date, and you may not be ready for this transition after just one meeting. It also raises the awkward question of who will pay. Yet if you both strongly enjoy a certain recreational activity, for instance, it's more comfortable to suggest doing that at your first meeting, and it's more natural to assume you'll each cover your own cost. And then you have something to do that's not so clearly considered a date, yet still gives your relationship a chance to grow.

One couple I know, who met through an online dating service, discovered they both had a passion for bird watching. Within a day or two after their first meeting, they were off on a birding jaunt together. It seemed to be one of several things that helped their relationship take off, and now, after more than a year, they're still together and engaged.

Consider whether you enjoy a pursuit like this, or a pastime, or an urge to grow in a certain area, or a longing to develop a certain talent, or a passion for a certain cause, which can provide something for you to do with someone sharing that interest whom you meet online. Weigh this question carefully, for there are many possible shared interests that can provide this benefit. Some of these include—

- *A love for canoeing, swimming, hiking, biking, bowling, racquetball, tennis, golf, miniature golf, softball, or some other sport or recreational activity*
- *A similar religious background and interest in growing spiritually, providing the basis to visit each other's church, visit a new church together, or attend special events*
- *A passion for musical performing or composing, providing the basis for sharing ideas or jamming*
- *A love for reading novels, allowing you to attend lectures or book club meetings together*
- *A passion for a social cause, such as helping the homeless, allowing you to volunteer your services together or attend rallies*
- *A love for antiques, allowing shopping trips together*
- *A common interest in collecting stamps, coins, or some other item, allowing you to share collections and attend meetings with other enthusiasts*
- *A common interest in a craft, allowing you to share projects, attend meetings and related events.*

Alternate Strategy

What if you and the person you're pursuing online simply don't share any interest that provides a natural activity for you, yet you still feel drawn to this person enough to want to meet them? There's an alternate strategy that can work as well in some cases, where you purposely take on a significant interest of your online companion's.

Does he have a skill you would like to develop, for instance, or a hobby or pastime you would like to learn more about? Or can you arouse enough interest in this area for it to be a basis for spending time together?

Let's say he's an avid bowler. While you have never been an enthusiast, you still enjoy an evening of bowling for the social value. Tell him you would love to bowl with him, as long as he understands he'll outdistance you greatly, and that you would cherish the chance to learn from him and hone your skill. He'll be flattered. And you'll both benefit from the opportunity this casual time gives you to get to know each other better.

Or perhaps you're the avid bowler. And as you chat with your new friend, you find he's eager enough to sharpen his own skill that he would enjoy bowling with you. Invite him to do it; this strategy can, of course, work both ways.

It won't work in every case, to be sure. One of you has to be comfortable being in a subordinate, apprentice role, plus still have enough interest in the activity to make it a viable option for spending time together. Still, in many cases you'll find there is *something* the two of you can do together that provides both a fun activity plus, by default, a cherished opportunity to grow better acquainted.

Diversify Your Efforts

Keeping these suggestions in mind and following them as best you can will enhance your success through any online dating service, and increase the chance you'll find an excellent match. Remember that with this approach, as with any you might try, a certain number of tries may be necessary to merit a success, and so resilience and persistence are essential—as in any endeavor. And if there's any endeavor in human life where rejection should never be taken personally, it's online dating. If someone closes you before you have the chance to meet in person, they aren't rejecting *you*, but a *perception* of you that, by the very nature of Internet communication, is considerably askew of who you really are.

And if someone chooses after the first face-to-face meeting not to take the relationship further, remember that the online process has primed them from the beginning to come into this meeting with unreasonable expectations that quite possibly *no* mortal can meet. The person who is right for you will be willing, and even eager, to adjust their expectations to the bonafide human creature they find you to be, and will find in their heart a genuine care for you as a child of God.

God can bring this person to you through the Internet as well as through any means, and because this option is so readily available, it can make great sense to use it. I strongly recommend, though, that you not let online matching be your only strategy for finding someone to marry. It's too easy to get caught up and obsessed with it, even as one might with online gambling. And it can make you reclusive. Stay socially active as well, and give at least half of your mate-seeking energy to more conventional means. Being with people does far more to sharpen your social skills than online communicating can ever hope to do. It also greatly increases the chance that others will look out for you and seek to help you. Pursue online matching during your down time, when you're not likely to be socializing anyway. Diversifying your efforts like this will result in the best possible stewardship of your time, and increase the chance that a given step you take will suddenly bring the prize you're seeking.

Fourteen

* * * * * * * * * *

Dating 101

AT SOME POINT IN YOUR SEARCH FOR SOMEONE TO marry, dating will likely be part of the process. You may indeed need to date often in this quest. My purpose in this chapter is to clarify when and why dating is important, and to advise you about getting it started with someone. Once it's in motion, and typically after the second or third date—when it's clear the two of you want to continue seeing each other—the how-tos of dating become much less vexing. The direction it takes for you as a couple at this point depends largely on your preferences, and you'll naturally seek opportunities to see each other that work best for you both. Once a relationship starts to work, in other words, dating tends to take care of itself and stops being such a glaring issue.

It's the initial stage—when you're trying to decide whether to date someone, how to break the ice, and how to approach that first date or two—that's so awkward for so many of us. And so it's this early phase of launching a dating relationship that I want to help you with in this chapter.

You may or may not need this help. You may be someone who isn't nervous about dating at all and instinctively approaches it well. And some fortunate couples fall into such a natural lockstep from the start that they readily look for any and every chance to be together. Their desire to see each other is so strong that dating occurs spontaneously as the natural result. They don't need anyone telling them how to go about dating.

In most cases, though, the process isn't fully natural, and may seem anything but. Indeed, the challenges can seem formidable. One of you needs to initiate dating, and compellingly enough that the other wants to accept. And one or both of you may use dating as a stage to court the other, and persuade that person that you're a worthy prospect for marriage. The thought of trying to accomplish that may feel like the challenge of a lifetime.

In America and most cultures, the man most often initiates a first date. In certain cases, it makes great sense for a woman to do it, and in the next chapter I'll offer guidance to women for taking initiative with men. But a man should usually assume this burden is on his shoulders, and most of the advice in this chapter is directed to men. (If a woman who you want to date does ask you out first, consider yourself very fortunate; but don't count on this happening.)

I urge men and women both to think of dating as a step toward *finding someone to marry*, and to date someone only if you believe there's at least a chance you would be interested in marrying this person. A man may know in his heart that he wouldn't possibly consider marrying a certain woman, and yet still ask her out and entertain her lavishly, hoping for a romantic spin with her. And he may indeed win her over and accomplish his goal. Yet he also loses valuable time he could be investing in his search for marriage. And he diminishes both himself and the one he dates when scoring is his sole motivation for asking her out.

A woman may also date for this reason. And a woman or man may date mainly from boredom, loneliness, habit, or simply wanting something to fill their time. Yet any time you date someone whom you know you wouldn't marry, you work against your goal of finding a spouse. Life isn't infinite, time is precious, and you should use your dating time as wisely as possible.

What Is Dating?

It helps to be as clear in your mind as possible about what dating is, why it's important, and what benefits it may bring you in searching for a mate. Dating is one of three general ways you may get to know someone through spending time with them.

Seeing each other routinely. You may grow acquainted with someone—up to a point—because work, church, or some other activity often brings you together. Without trying, you frequently see him because you work in the same office, sit near each other at church, or ride the same commuter train. You can often nurture these situations somewhat to improve your opportunity: you purposely sit next to her at the office lunch, linger to chat with him after the church service, save her a seat next to you on the train.

If your relationship is to grow, though, you'll need to start seeing each other outside of the default situation at some point. You need greater privacy than it provides to grow a deeper friendship, and more leisurely time to share freely and intimately. The symbolism of it is important as well: the fact that you both agree to make special time to be together signals that yours is more than just a casual friendship. Also, in most routine settings you see the other mainly on his best time. It takes more extended, unstructured time to discover her rougher edges, and to understand what "warts and all" means in her case.

Hanging out. Hanging out is the next possible step in getting acquainted. You may bypass it and jump directly to dating someone you've been getting to know at work or elsewhere, or even someone you've just met. But hanging out often provides a more relaxed way to test the waters and still enjoy some significant private or semi-private time together.

The key distinctive of hanging out is that neither of you regards it as dating, but simply as logging time together as friends. You avoid the trappings of dating, too—no candlelight dinners or moonlight cruises. Typically, you do things with your opposite-sex friend you would just as readily do with a same-sex friend or by yourself. And if any cost is involved, you each cover yourself. Physical intimacy isn't part of it. And others may sometimes join you in your "hang time" as well.

In spite of these boundaries, by hanging out you signal to each other that you see your friendship as something special and on a different level from other acquaintances. It's also permissible for either or both of you to cherish the hope that hanging out may eventually lead to something more, or provide the opportunity to determine if you want to advance to a more serious relationship.

Dating. The major difference between dating and hanging out is that by asking someone out, or by accepting a date, you're indicating at least potential interest in getting serious with this person. That, at least, is the ideal way of looking at it, and the one I urge you to respect if you're genuine in your desire to find a spouse. Of course, people date for many reasons that fall short of this ideal, but that is counterproductive in your search for someone to marry.

While you may choose to double date occasionally or to join with a group of couples for an outing, dating, much more typically than hanging out, is a private affair where the two of you deliberately spend time together by yourselves. And again, like it or not, and in spite of many advances in gender equality in recent decades, cultural expectations about dating have not changed greatly, and most men and women assume that the man will be the first to initiate it. So while I'll look at exceptions to this rule, I'm addressing men more directly in this chapter.

I urge you as a man to think of dating as a step, and usually an essential one, in *courting* a woman. When you think of dating, think of it as part of *courting*. The vocabulary we use to describe to ourselves and others what we do affects us more profoundly than we usually realize. "Courting" is one of those nearly forgotten terms that, when you embrace it and lock in to it as the basis for taking interest in a woman, naturally gears your behavior in the right direction and helps clarify the choices you have to make.

To Date or Not to?

The first question to resolve when a woman attracts you is whether to seek to date her, hang out, or leave well enough alone. Here I think you'll find the word courting can help you turn this corner. Are you comfortable putting this stake in the ground and, by asking her for a date, implying you're at least potentially interested in courting her? Are you comfortable with her possibly perceiving your motivation this way? If you don't feel ready yet to send this message, then consider looking for ways to hang out first, or continue taking advantage of any natural opportunity you have for getting to know her. As I've noted, hanging out—by pursuing an activity you both enjoy—is often the ideal step to take with someone you've met online, especially if you're adjusting your expectations considerably once you meet in person. Logging this casual time allows you to get to know your online companion better, before deciding whether to elevate the relationship to dating.

If you do feel ready to date her, you don't need to be certain she'll accept before asking her out. Indeed, you don't need to be confident or optimistic about it. A healthy willingness to risk is essential to entering the dating field, without which you'll remain forever stuck in the inertia of singleness. There are just two cautions to keep in mind.

Persistence with a given woman is admirable to a certain point, and may help to win her over. But you don't want to cross the subtle line where she begins to perceive you as pesky. I advise a three-strikes rule: If she turns you down three times without asking for a "rain check," then you should let her go. You've shown enough interest in her by now, and you'll likely come off as needy or insensitive if you try again. This is the time to leave it in the Lord's hands and hers, and assume that if there's any future with her, she'll take the initiative to let you know. Barring that happening, and soon, you should move on and seek a new opportunity.

The second caution is to consider how asking her out might change the nature of your friendship if she should turn you down. Again, you need a strong willingness to risk. Your purpose isn't to stockpile female friendships but to find someone to marry, and eventually winning that prize will compensate for possibly losing a friendship or two along the way. But you don't want to be foolhardy either. If you believe that someone who's a strong and important friend to you is likely to turn you down if you ask her out, and that broaching it would damage your friendship, then don't do it. Many friendships *can* endure talk of dating even if the woman doesn't accept, so pray about it, and follow your best judgment.

With these cautions in mind, the next question is how to ask her out. Not long ago, you would have been limited to phoning her, asking in person, or writing a letter. Each of these was a *respectful* method, which served suitors well in different situations. Today, your communication options have increased dramatically. In addition to the traditional three, they include e-mail, instant messaging, Facebook, texting, and voicemail. Any of these methods is fine to confirm details of a date you've arranged. And as your relationship grows, you may agree to use any of them for arranging times together.

But you're in a unique position asking for that first date. Then, more than any other time, you want to convey to her that you would be *honored* for her to accept. If you think of this date as possibly the start of courting, then it puts the question in clearer perspective. You wouldn't consider proposing to her by e-mail or any informal electronic means, would you? Then you shouldn't use such a method to request a first date either.

Just how formal, then, should you be? Of course you can overdo it; sending her an engraved invitation will compel her immediately to file a restraining order. And writing her a letter, while once common, is usually too stilted today. The key is simply to *talk* to her directly. Phoning her, or asking her in person when you have an unrushed moment, conveys the proper respect and the sense that you would be honored to have this special time with her.

Do make one nod to modern communication. If when you ask her, you sense she feels awkward and not certain how to reply, tell her please just to think about it and e-mail you her response, if that's easiest. Giving her the freedom to e-mail you rather than phone may spell relief for her, for it conveys you're not going to be difficult. It will be easier for her to say no, if that's her decision, by e-mail, and perhaps to more honestly admit the reason. But a yes from her by e-mail is also a great encouragement for you. It's highly likely to be sincere, since she has had more chance to measure her thoughts than often is possible in conversation.

Give her, in short, the option to respond by e-mail, but talk to her directly when you first ask her out.

The First Date
In deciding what to ask her to do with you, thinking of this date as possibly the start of courting helps to narrow your options. You want to do something conveying respect for her, that you're honored by her company, and that you value it above anyone else's for this special time you're together. These goals clearly rule out many options. She'll be less than impressed if you take her to hang out with you and your male buddies at the sports bar, or tag her along to watch you bowl in the Friday night league, or escort her to dinner at the local Tastee Freeze. Unless there's a compelling reason to double date or join in some group activity, you should choose an option allowing substantial private time together.

Here there's another principle you should follow. Simply stated: Overdo it *somewhat*—enough to flatter and affirm her—but not so much that you make her uncomfortable. Strive to exceed her expectations, in other words. But don't choose an option so lavish and expensive that she feels you're trying too hard to impress her, or that she's unfairly obliged to repay you, or that the event is more important to you than the time with her.

If you take her to dinner, for instance, choose a nice restau-

rant—one that qualifies as "fine dining." But, if you live in a metropolitan area offering some very expensive upper-crust dining
spots, avoid such a place for the first date, even if you can afford it.
She'll not be as relaxed in that environment. It may even be a deal
killer if she thinks you've gone beyond reasonable limits to win her
favor. Save the five-star palace for a later date, like the night you
propose!

Speaking of dinner, it's the option I most often recommend for
a first date. It's a safe choice the vast majority of the time, for most
women love being taken to a nice restaurant, and many are flattered by the invitation. You both get to enjoy a good meal. And
providing you choose the restaurant carefully (not too noisy, tables
reasonably spaced), the atmosphere naturally inspires extended, supportive conversation. If you're hoping for a significant chance to
talk with her, then it's hard to go wrong with this option. Many
great relationships have launched in just this setting.

Choosing the right restaurant can pose a certain challenge. You
want to show initiative and creativity. Yet you don't want to choose
a place she might dislike. A plush, white tablecloth Chinese restaurant may be ideal—*if* she loves Chinese. If she doesn't, you're in
for an uneasy evening. Keep in mind that no matter how top-rated
any international restaurant is, some people cannot gastronomically
handle its food (excepting, of course, people from that country—
and if she is, then it may be a perfect choice.) Some are allergic to
seafood as well. You shouldn't start by asking her where she wants
to go, for that puts her in an awkward position. She'll likely choose
an option less than her favorite, out of respect for your wallet and
not wanting to appear greedy. Asking her first can also suggest you
haven't given much thought to it. You want to convey a good balance of initiative and sensitivity to her needs.

Generally, you're on safest ground to suggest a nice American
restaurant with a good variety of dinner options. Or take a middle
ground: If you're in a metropolitan area with numerous choices,
and you personally enjoy most food, research the best international

options available. When you ask her out, tell her you're thinking of going to Joe's Steak and Shrimp Palace. But then ask her if she's a major fan of any other country's food. She'll probably respond no and that Joe's is perfect. But if she confesses that she craves Thai food, for instance, be ready with a good Thai restaurant to suggest. If you haven't been to one before, be honest in admitting so; but tell her you would love the experience, and say so sincerely. She'll enjoy being the authority on this cuisine, and flattered that you trust her judgment about it.

Normally, you should tell her where you plan to take her, and not leave it a surprise, so she'll know how to dress. She'll probably enjoy studying the menu online as well. If she has dietary issues, she'll be much more relaxed if she can confirm that the restaurant has dinner options that work for her. If you do know her well enough to know she likes being surprised, and are certain she'll like the place you've chosen, then you can tell her it's a surprise—but let her know you're going to somewhere nice. If you two aren't well acquainted, then don't risk this option. Some women are offended if a man they don't know well wants to surprise them. Even though your intentions may be golden, it can strike the woman as presumptuous, and she may feel disrespected if you don't divulge your plans to her in advance.

If you aren't confident you two are ready for an evening of chatting, then opt for an event rather than dinner for the first date. But choose a classy event that requires some expenditure on your part, and one where you are spectators, not participants, and can expect to be nicely entertained. A play or concert is usually a good option. A movie can be also, if your city sports a high-end vintage theater featuring a single film. Avoid the local cineplex, though, which is too chaotic and lowbrow for a first date. A professional sporting event can be a fine choice, if you know she likes the sport—or if the event by its nature is classy, such as a golf or tennis tournament, or a polo match.

Whatever the event, obtain tickets in advance if possible, and

take any step that makes the logistics easier and shows thoughtful-
ness on your part. If valet parking is available, by all means use it.
The expense isn't great, and she'll appreciate the courtesy—especially if it's a long walk from the parking lot.

Whether you invite her to dinner or an event, plan on paying for
her—and insist on it if she should suggest paying for herself. Use
language that clearly indicates you plan to treat her. "May I take
you to dinner Saturday night?", for instance, as opposed to "Can
we have dinner together Saturday?"—which leaves open the option of who pays. If you don't get it right at first, be sure to inject
somewhere in the conversation that you're looking forward to *taking her* to dinner. Don't leave her with any doubt that you intend to
pay. But, if you're taking her to an event, avoid language like, "I
have two tickets for the Redskins game—will you go with me?"
That may leave her wondering if you were given the tickets and are
simply asking her as a convenience—in other words, not greatly
different from hanging out. Instead, just ask her if she will go with
you to the game, and add that you would love for her to be your
guest.

Other Particulars . . .

Let's look at some other specifics of the first date. The overdo-it-
but-moderately principle helps clarify what to do in most of these
matters.

Grooming. Wherever you're planning to go, consider the range
of ways men dress there, and go for the classier end; just don't
dress *so* classy that you're out of place and call attention to yourself. If you're taking her to a nice restaurant, check to see if it has a
dress code, and if so, follow it carefully. If a sports jacket is required, yet you show up without one, the maitre d' may provide
you one to wear—embarrassing, to say the least, and it's not likely
to fit you well. Wearing a sports jacket to a restaurant, even if not
required, is a good idea in any case, along with dress khakis or
equivalent, a colored shirt, and nice shoes. But skip the tie, unless

the place requires it.

The sports jacket may be too much for an arena concert, but ideal to wear to a play at a nice theater (and if it's really upscale, like The Kennedy Center or Carnegie Hall, then the tie fits as well). Again, consider the venue and how other men are likely to dress, and choose among the classier options.

Observe impeccable hygiene. Get a haircut within a few days of the date, unless your hairstyle doesn't recommend it. If you tend to be sloppy about shaving and often sport a few days' overgrowth, shave on the day of your date, but not so close to the time that your face is still red. Cut ear hairs if you have them (something most men overlook), and check your face for stray hairs, which can be annoying. Unless you know she's allergic to fragrance—or you are—wear a light cologne. Brush your teeth about an hour before the date, and rinse with water well; but don't use a mouthwash then or breath mints afterwards. You don't want your breath to smell like you've hygiened it, in other words, you just don't want it to smell bad. If you smoke, don't do so between brushing your teeth and picking her up; climb a wall if you have to, but don't smoke then.

Paying. This rule is simple. Plan on paying for everything during the evening. Food, parking, transportation, event. Cover it all. If she offers to help with a tip or anything else, thank her, but assure her you have it covered. The only exception would be if you happen to shop together during the evening—the restaurant is in a hotel, for instance, and you browse in the gift shop. Then it's fine to let her buy some item she wants for herself. If it's something inexpensive, though, you might offer to cover it also—follow your instincts there.

Transportation. Plan to handle all transportation for the evening. Clean your car inside and out before the date. Run it through a professional car wash or wash it yourself. Remove all litter and clutter. And make sure it's fueled sufficiently that you won't have to stop for gas during the evening (which would show you hadn't prepared well; gassing up also leaves your hands smelly). If you don't drive or prefer not to, then hire a taxi to pick you up first, then her. When moving between events (from dinner to a movie, for instance), choose a taxi over public transportation, even though it costs more, unless the convenience of public transportation clearly outweighs it. But cover her cost for any subway or bus jaunt.

If you live in the city and drive, but don't maintain a car for economic reasons, then renting a Zipcar may be preferable to a taxi, depending on the amount of driving you expect to do and how much flexibility you want. Just be sure to choose one of Zipcar's nicer model options.

Being a gentleman. Be alert to providing gentlemanly courtesies for her throughout the evening. Open the car door for her, and check to be sure her coat or dress is fully inside before closing it. When you arrive at your destination, open the car door for her again; if she jumps out too quickly to do that, at least make the effort to close it for her. Open doors for her throughout the evening, and let her walk through first. Hold the chair for her at the restaurant. Let her order all things first—drinks, dinner, dessert. At a concert or any event where you sit, let her enter the row and sit down first. Walk her to her door when you arrive home.

Yes, this is all very old school, I understand, and I realize that occasionally some women are offended by such gentlemanliness and consider it a power play. Most, I assure you, are not and truly appreciate it. Remember, you are looking for *someone to marry*. So consider whether you would want to marry a woman who takes offense at such common and long-accepted manly courtesies. If that doesn't bother you, and you know she would be offended by these gestures, then adjust your behavior accordingly. Otherwise, take the risk of being a gentleman; usually, it pays off handsomely.

Conversation. Your best opportunity during the evening for making a positive impression on the woman you're dating comes through the single dynamic of conversation. Indeed, through it, you may succeed in turning the heart of someone who is skeptical about you into someone who admires you, and even more. The key, though, lies in your ability to take a sincere and meaningful interest *in her*— her history, her present, her dreams for the future.

We men too often suppose that to succeed in love, we need to be master talkers. It's important, we assume, to keep her entertained with jokes and funny stories. And vital to share as much as we can about ourselves, and to "humbly" interject as many notable facts about our life as possible. Also helpful to impress her with our grasp of different issues we believe are important. Oh, and critical—if she should speak of a problem or issue she's facing, to provide an insightful *solution*!

This belief that we must be an impressive talker is the most unfortunate assumption we men carry into dating and courting, and in some cases it's outright tragic. One reason it's sad is that it causes us to feel under pressure throughout the evening to be interesting and entertaining. That, in turn, positions us to come off like we're trying too hard. It also can work against the one thing that will most succeed in winning her heart, which, again, is taking an interest in her. That, by definition, means bridling our inclination to talk to some degree. The best-kept secret of successful dating is that we'll come off far better if we prove to her that we're a good listener than a good talker.

How much should you talk? How important is it to be interesting and entertaining? Well, she'll like it if you show a sense of humor—up to a point, and providing it's appropriate. Life is full of absurdities, and spontaneous funny remarks about the situations you're in together can be endearing. Just be careful not to overdo it, and avoid comments that are unkind to others or display veiled hate or anger on your part. Some light teasing of others can be fine, if she's comfortable with it, and poking fun at yourself is usually a winner.

Keep teasing of her to a bare minimum, if at all. If you don't know her well, it may come off as criticism, even if you're trying to be loving. Humor, in short, should be sensitive to her, her sensibilities and values. If a joke you're thinking of telling might be offensive to her, for all the world, don't tell it. It could be a deal killer on the spot. If you like to tell jokes, keep it to two or three during the evening, and only if they have at least some bearing on the situation. Tell too many jokes, and you'll come off as one who's more concerned about entertaining than with getting to know her.

One other thing on humor: If you're a frequent punner by habit, bridle that instinct, my friend. Constant punning is flat-out annoying to most people, and conveys insecurity. An occasional pun that's truly fitting to the situation can be great, but keep it to that.

She'll definitely want to learn about you—your past, present, and aspirations. Some talk of your accomplishments is important, just keep it balanced. Be equally willing to talk about your failures. She'll respect you for that and will be relieved, for it helps her feel on an equal playing field with you. Just be careful not to come off as whiney or self-pitying. Be as positive as you can in speaking about your mistakes; stress what you've learned from them and your hope for a better future. And as with your accomplishments, don't let your failures be the central focus of the evening's conversation.

Let *her* be that central focus. Let talk about yourself flow naturally with the conversation's give-and-take. Start things off by asking her a probing question or two about herself: "Where did you grow up?" "Where have you lived?" "How do you like living here?" As you show interest in her, she'll naturally return the favor by asking about you—hopefully!—and at that point, share freely and joyfully. But be restrained also, and don't get carried away, as we men too easily do. After speaking for a moment about your experience, find a way to direct the conversation back to her. After talking for a minute or two about your love for the drama club in high school, simply stop and ask her, "what was *your* favorite part of high school—did you have one?"

Keep this sort of ebb and flow going throughout the evening, and you'll succeed well in holding her interest, both in you and in divulging her life to you. If such give-and-take doesn't come naturally to you, spend some time before the date thinking through creative, appropriate questions to ask her. Then be alert to her responses to "iceberg statements" that give you a basis for further questions. If she mentions that she spent her early years in Pittsburgh, for instance, but then her family moved to Topeka when she was thirteen, ask her whether the move was difficult or welcome. Which city did she like more? And why? Each answer she gives provides a lead for further questions, so just keep prodding her, trusting she'll turn the attention back to you when she has had a fair chance to share.

If you already know her well, then of course such basic getting acquainted questions are beside the point. But this sort of give-and-take with her is still critically important, and will make the differ-ence between keeping her interest and leaving her with eyes glazing over. Pry her about recent events in her life, about anything that interests her or you—providing it doesn't *amount* to prying. That is, steer clear of any area she considers private (and if you accidentally tread there, quickly tread out by graciously changing the subject). This conversational back-and-forth is also by far the best approach if you're getting to know her in a less formal way than dating, through hanging out or chatting at work or elsewhere. But if you've tended to dominate the conversation in the past, use the date as an opportunity to demonstrate (and hopefully launch) a more gentlemanly conversational style.

Issues of the day and countless other topics can provide meat for your conversation as well. Before your date, identify a half-dozen or so current news items everyone is talking about. Clarify your perspective on them. Then, if there's a lull in the conversation, ask her for her thoughts on one of them. If she's not familiar with it or not interested, try another. Be ready to jump in with your own thoughts too. Most important, though, if she shows interest in a topic, draw her out on what she thinks, and express appreciation for her viewpoint.

If you're both Christian, or of the same faith, there are many spiritual, theological, and philosophical topics you may naturally talk about. Just—again—be sure to give her at least equal time to elaborate her thoughts, no matter how knowledgeable you may be on the matter. If you differ from her on an issue, be honest in saying that, but do so graciously, showing as much appreciation as you can for her viewpoint. Above all else, don't be argumentative but be supportive in discussing any topic or issue. Use the conversation as a chance to demonstrate that you're congenial, not contentious, and comfortable agreeing to disagree with others. Show her that friendship is far more important to you than needing to be right on some issue.

There is, of course, another major conversation area that may indeed be your primary one for the evening—depending on things between you at the moment—and that's your relationship itself, your future, and the possibility of marriage. There's enough to say about such serious talk that I'll devote the next chapter to it. If you're on a first date with someone you don't know well, though, don't be too hasty to talk about your relationship *per se*. Put the emphasis on getting acquainted for now, and put off more serious talk till the second or third date at the earliest. Asking her thoughts on marriage in general, though—about whether she wants to marry or stay single—and sharing your own, is usually quite appropriate and often recommended. More on that in a moment.

Flowers? Showing up with flowers in your hand for a first date is a great idea, as it is on occasion for any date. For the first date with a new acquaintance, though, keep it a simple, not hugely expensive assortment, and a bright, cheerful mix. Flowers make a statement, and overdoing it with flowers will embarrass her and make you appear presumptuous. If you don't know her well, avoid roses of any sort; they signify romantic affection, which you two are well-shy of expressing to each other (a rose or two in a general assortment is fine, though). Providing flowers already cut in a vase is considerate for an ill person, hospital patient, or someone bereaving, but it's overdoing it for a first date. Simply bring them with the stems wrapped in paper, and let the flower shop handle that part. Remember, too, that their employee is trained to know what's appropriate for the occasion. Tell her that you need a simple assortment for a first date, and she may have the perfect idea.

Physical Intimacy
The possibility of being physically intimate with someone you're dating is usually highly enticing. Yet that prospect can also be intimidating, especially if you don't know her well or have never been affectionate with her before. I recall on certain dates as a young man feeling pressured to demonstrate I could be an outstanding lover. It was a matter of proving my manhood, and I was certain that drawing her into physical intimacy was essential to winning her heart. You may feel similarly stressed and worried about how to initiate physical affection. Indeed, such "performance anxiety" is the most potent fear many men suffer in the early stage of dating.

Fortunately, you have good cause to relax, and for two important reasons. One is, again, the simple fact that your primary goal in dating this person isn't to score physically but to court her. You want to win her hand for marriage, or at least seriously consider that possibility with her. If you two truly are well matched for marriage, then physical affection will likely break out spontaneously at some point. Your mutual desire for it will be strong enough that it will simply ignite. One of you may do something to initiate it, but if won't have to be major. The mix of chemistry, companionship, and trust that you enjoy will be enough to enkindle it.

In fact, the usual challenge in a healthy, developing relationship isn't how to spark physical affection, but how to keep it within reasonable bounds. Its failure to develop after a reasonable time— and especially after one of you has shown interest—is a good sign you aren't matched for marriage. If either of you has to force it or try too hard to persuade the other, it isn't a good sign.

The second reason is that on your first few dates you do well to observe certain boundaries that completely remove the pressure to present yourself as a world-class lover. If you haven't been physically affectionate with her before, then light to *very* light is the best advice on the first date. Occasional gentle touching of her arm or hand during the evening is good to do, if she reciprocates. And a light hug and kiss (on the lips if she makes it easy, otherwise on the cheek) at the end of the evening is appropriate, if gentle touching has occurred during the date. But bridle any tendency to push it beyond this. She'll want to know that you're drawn to her more for her heart and personality than the chance to score physically, and your restraint at this time will impress her far more than pushing the limits.

Keeping it light for the next two or three dates is the best idea also. Your purpose during this time is to get acquainted, and you want to demonstrate that you're pursuing her from the highest possible motives.

As your relationship develops, expressing affection physically becomes more important. Since you're considering each other for marriage, you each need assurance that the other wants to be affectionate with you. At the same time, it's critical to respect each other's standards and boundaries, and to demonstrate that certain values are important to you personally.

You also are wisest to leave some new territory to enjoy and discover in marriage. If you choose to become fully intimate before then, marriage will be a less momentous and inviting step for you both. I understand well the arguments to the contrary. One commonly raised is that you shouldn't marry "for sex." If you don't let yourselves enjoy it all before marriage, in other words, you may be drawn into marrying by your sexual need, even though your match isn't good.

There's no question that sex is too great a lure for some who marry. Yet far more people, in my observation, suffer from the opposite problem. They lose the zest to marry because they're already enjoying all the sexual benefits outside of it. Here we simply need to be honest about human psychology. No matter how greatly we may want to marry, nor how much we would benefit, it's still an intimidating step for many of us. We need as much positive incentive as possible to encourage us to take the leap, and to help us perceive marriage not just as a step toward maturity but *a prize*. The anticipation of greater sexual intimacy is a healthy incentive to marry if other factors in your relationship are right. And, depending on your makeup, it may be a necessary part of the mix of motivations that persuade you to marry. Even if not, you still do yourself and your partner a wonderful favor by leaving some fresh experience to look forward to on the wedding night, honeymoon, and beyond.

Another reason often argued for full sexual intimacy before marriage is the importance of testing the waters, to find if the two of you are truly compatible sexually. The notion of "sexual compatibility" underlying such experimentation, though, is largely a myth. Any man and woman who are at least moderately attracted to each other sexually, and are compassionate, supportive individuals, have the potential of building a fulfilling sexual relationship. And moderate involvement is all that's needed to ensure that this basic attraction is there. Mystery, in fact, is one of the greatest sexual enticements. If you deplete your relationship's reserve of mystery before marriage, you may go into marriage feeling less sexually compatible than you would otherwise.

Just how physically intimate you should allow yourselves to be prior to marriage is a question different couples will answer differently, in light of their wishes and values. It's something the two of you should carefully discuss and agree on, before letting intimacy escalate out of hand. I strongly recommend agreeing, at minimum, to stay fully clothed before marriage. While this will take some discipline, the benefit is you'll leave a whole new, wonderful world of sexual bliss to discover together once married. I also recommend Lewis Smedes' *Sex for Christians: The Limits and Liberties of Sexual Living,* as required reading at this stage (or before, so you'll be prepared). It provides insightful guidance for navigating the physical relationship during this intermediate period.

My purpose in this book is to help you find someone to marry, rather than to explore all the particulars of growing a relationship, which would make this book hopelessly long. So my main concern is to give you guidance for the early stage of the physical relationship, while your relationship itself is just developing. And here my advice is twofold.

First, while one of you may need to make some effort to initiate physical affection, it shouldn't have to be major. If this relationship truly has the potential to end in marriage, then neither of you should have to try too hard to induce the other to be affectionate. You may find that physical expression simply ignites spontaneously. But if it hasn't by the fifth date or so, yet light touching has been common—and perhaps an occasional light kiss—then it may be advisable to take a strategic step to encourage greater physical affection between you. I recommend this step *if* other factors in your relationship are developing well and you're finding yourself seriously open to marrying her. If so, then at an appropriate time during the date, when you have the privacy, initiate a warm kiss—one that lasts a few seconds. If she doesn't resist, and especially if she responds enthusiastically, then try another.

If that kiss is met with equal enthusiasm, then—secondly—use this moment of physical intimacy as a pretext *to talk*. Take the opportunity to talk specifically about your physical relationship and the direction it should take. She'll likely be extremely grateful you've brought the matter into the open and made it comfortable to talk about, and any awkwardness either of you feels should fade quickly. The direction this discussion takes will depend upon how much you've talked already about your relationship itself—if at all. If this is the first time, then let the matter of physical intimacy be the basis for a more general conversation about your future. Then, in that general context, talk also about your physical relationship.

If you have already had some serious discussion about your relationship before this date, then let this kissing episode be the entrée to talk specifically about your physical relationship itself.

If she resists your effort to kiss her, or responds less than enthusiastically, don't lose heart just yet. If you've already had some discussion about your relationship, and she has said she wants to get serious, then she probably wants to talk about the physical part also, and to have some clear understanding about it before you become more expressive. Explain to her that you would love to be more affectionate with her, and ask for her thoughts about it. If she merely needs to talk, then a positive discussion about physical intimacy should ensue, where you can be clear to each other about your wishes and boundaries.

If you haven't talked about your relationship at all before, then this is when you should. She may be very open to physical intimacy, but first wants to know your intentions for the relationship itself. Stay optimistic and hopeful for the moment. Explain to her that you tried to kiss her because you're yearning for a more serious relationship with her, and are open to considering marriage. I'll offer more guidance on launching serious conversation about your relationship in the next chapter. And I'll look at how to proceed if your effort to kiss her sparks a less encouraging discussion, where she tells you she isn't interested in getting serious, or needs some time to consider it.

If, at the other extreme, physical affection develops spontaneously before you've talked at all about your relationship, what then? Even if it's your first date, catch your breath before it goes very far and tell her you need to talk. She'll respect you greatly for taking control. If you know for certain you would like a more serious relationship, where you consider each other for marriage, then tell her so. If you're not at that point, or she responds that she isn't, then— as difficult as it may be—put the breaks on the physical part for now. Don't let it run ahead of the relationship itself. Let it always be an expression of commitment that is truly there and clearly expressed between you. Don't allow her any pretext for thinking you're simply using her.

How Persistent Should You Be?

We've been talking about strategies for establishing a dating relationship with a woman you are interested in courting, or potentially so. The question remains, just how persistent should you be in seeking the opportunity to date someone? When should you accept her no as truly "no," and when "not yet"?

No matter how greatly you want to date a certain woman, nor how strongly you're attracted to her, it's important to keep in mind that you're on a mission to find someone to marry, and she may or may not be right for you. Unless you have a clear standard for determining when to cut your losses, you may persist way beyond a reasonable point chasing someone unavailable, and lose valuable time. It's for this reason I recommend the three-strikes rule I've spoken of earlier.

First, though, the *one*-strike rule. If a woman turns you down without explanation, or shows contempt or disrespect for you in any way, don't push it any further. Accept her no graciously, but don't pursue any further contact. Whatever her rude reply implies, it demonstrates she isn't someone you should consider marrying. Don't be tempted from pride or passion to try again. This isn't a game of triumphing over difficult odds, but a mission to find a partner for marriage, and she has proven unworthy. Countless other prospects are out there, and so focus on finding one who is interested in you *and* a considerate person.

Let me hasten to assure you that it's most unlikely any woman ever will respond to you so abruptly. In my single years—roughly a dozen years of actively dating—I received plenty of nos, but all were courteous—every last one. And it's only rarely that I've heard of someone being turned down rudely. So don't obsess about this happening, and by all means don't let this concern keep you from trying.

Now the three-strikes rule. Fortunately, it's not complicated. If you make three reasonable attempts to ask her out and she turns them all down, even though graciously, drop it at this point. Drop it even if her reasons for declining have all seemed reasonable extenuating circumstances. By the third time, assume more is going on beneath the surface. Trust God's providence that these three nos show it's not in your best interest to keep pursuing her. Trust equally that if you've judged incorrectly, she'll find a way to let you know she wants another chance. Indeed, assume that if the relationship does have potential, your backing off will do more to spark her interest than your continued persistence.

Allow at least one-to-two weeks between each date request. You can make the second sooner if there's a compelling reason—an event you believe she'll enjoy that you have to secure tickets for soon, for instance. But don't try this strategy for the third request; definitely leave some buffer between efforts two and three.

An exception to the three-strikes rule: If she tells you pointedly that she wants a rain check, and shows eagerness for you to try again, then by all means keep the option open. Trying another time or two is certainly justified in this case. But if she fails to show obvious interest in your asking again, that's equally significant. And if she turns you down three times without clearly asking for a further opportunity, then you should move on.

Follow the three-strikes rule the first time you ask a woman out and, if needed, the second and third. I say "if needed," for as your relationship grows, you can feel freer to ask her directly if she wants to keep dating, or whether declining a date means her interest has waned. You can then decide whether to continue asking her based on a clear understanding of where things stand. I offer the three-strikes rule for when you ask out a new acquaintance or someone you don't know well. Then it would be disrespectful to ask her why she has turned you down. She may choose to offer an explanation. But apart from that, take three nos as final, and don't press her for details. Whatever disappointment you may feel, enjoy the fact that you're not responsible to implore her for more information. Think of it as a burden lifted and an option clarified, and now turn your attention to looking for someone new.

Keep in mind that by trying too hard with this woman—even just by dwelling on your disappointment with her too much—you may be keeping yourself from someone out there who will be attracted to you and is much better suited for you. Trade this discouraging situation for the hope of finding one where the energy and momentum is positive. Indeed, looking forward and not back is vital to the attitude of heart that will move you toward finding someone to marry.

Fifteen

* * * * * * * * * *

Serious Talk and Deciding About Marriage

JAZZ ICON DAVE BRUBECK HAS ENJOYED A REMARKABLY happy and successful marriage. His wife Iola has been his constant companion and supporter, and a spirit of friendship and partnership has prevailed between them. She has co-authored songs with him, managed his career, and along the way they've managed to raise four children, all now professional musicians. Today, as Brubeck approaches his 90th year and his marriage its 68th, Iola continues to accompany him on his frequent tours.

Here's the most interesting part: Dave and Iola met on a blind date while attending the same college. *And* they decided to marry that same night. The story gets even more interesting: "It was his musically gifted mother who . . . insisted that David go to the College (now University) of the Pacific, and, once there, worried he was becoming a hermit. Take a girl to a dance, she said. Brubeck

asked his roommate which girl was the brightest, and then he sent
the roommate to approach Iola Whitlock. After some dancing . . .
David suggested they just talk. After three hours, they had decided
to get married."[16]

I love this story, for it shows how serious discussion about marriage can erupt spontaneously and unexpectedly, with someone you
barely know, even on a first date. A decision to marry can even take
place under such circumstances. And the intuition that can function
then is sometimes surprisingly accurate, and as reliable as a decision reached carefully after a long courtship. Of course it doesn't
always happen this way, and of course Brubeck's example is extreme. Yet it's not *that* extreme, given that serious talk about marriage often does ignite quickly and naturally when you've met the
right person.

Here, again, is a message of hope for any of us who fear the
mountain we must climb to find someone to marry is impossibly
steep, or the time we must invest impossibly great. We're reminded
how rapidly a new relationship can accelerate, and how profoundly
things can change in a single day. I doubt that when Dave Brubeck
woke that morning he had any inkling that by bedtime, he would
have taken a step forever radically improving his life. Any of us
who are ever tempted to despair in our search for marriage should
remember this story, and take heart that we don't know what a given
day will bring, nor the difference meeting someone new will make.
We're reminded of the importance of keeping our life in motion,
staying active socially, making new acquaintances—*and* seeking
others' help wherever we can. Brubeck may have had to swallow
hard to ask his roommate's assistance in meeting Iola, but now, 67
years later, he still enjoys the benefits of that one humble effort.

Brubeck's example also shows that talking about marriage is
achievable, even for those of us who don't imagine ourselves
"skilled" at it—and this brings us to the purpose of this chapter. I
want to look now at how you can initiate discussion about marriage
with someone, and at what strategies are best to keep in mind. But

it's important to begin with this note of hope, for the thought of broaching this topic can seem the most intimidating part of developing a serious relationship. In fact, it's often the easiest. And when your match is good, you may find chatting about marriage to be as natural as talking about last night's episode of American Idol.

If it doesn't come quite so naturally, this doesn't mean you aren't well matched, but may simply indicate that one or both of you are shy or reserved enough that some breaking of the ice is needed. From my experience, about half the time it happens as it did for Dave and Iola—spontaneously, unpredictably, without much prompting on either's part. Your mutual attraction, the timing, and the setting all conspire to inspire you to start talking about marriage, and once that dam is broken, the discussion flows freely. In the other half of cases, one of you needs to strategically prime the pump a bit. The steps to initiate marriage talk, though, are not difficult, and these are what I want to look at now. (I'm addressing men primarily in the following section, and women in the next.)

When it's a New Relationship

Let's look first at the case where you're dating a new, or fairly new, acquaintance. On the first date, it's usually a good idea to talk about marriage in general but not your relationship specifically. Ask her whether she hopes to marry or prefers staying single. After her response, tell her of your own wish to marry. As you open the door to this topic, you'll both probably talk about past experiences with family and marriage—what your parents' marriages were like, and how well certain friends or siblings have done in theirs. If either of you is divorced or widowed, you'll likely divulge at least something about that past marriage. The important thing at this point isn't to learn every possible detail about each other's past and outlook on marriage, but to get a good sense of each other's *interest* in marrying (or in marrying again).

If she strongly implies—or tells you straightforwardly—that she doesn't want to get married (or marry again), take her admission at face value. Be grateful you've discovered this critical detail about her on the first date. Resist the temptation to go on a mission to change her thinking about marriage, which normally is a high-risk endeavor. You have better things to do with your time en route to finding a partner, and you should let this relationship go in favor of looking for another.

If she indicates eagerness to marry, or seems reasonably open, then you've discovered something equally important about her, as she hopefully has about you on this first date.

If she does show interest in marrying, then wait till the fourth date to talk about your relationship itself and the possibility of a future together. Providing, that is, that this discussion doesn't evolve spontaneously before then. If it does, don't worry—it can be quite appropriate this early in some cases (like Brubeck's), and may arise unavoidably when you talk about marriage in general on the first date. But if not, wait till the fourth date before doing anything strategic to initiate it.

Proceed to the fourth date and this serious talk, though, only if you've resolved by now that you would like to court her for marriage. For the sake of best managing your time in your quest for someone to marry, I recommend after the third date taking what may seem like a monumental step of faith in trusting your instincts. In truth, you should know her well enough by now to determine if you want to seriously consider her for marriage. If in all honesty you don't want to, or are uncertain, then trust your judgment (or lack of it at this time). Don't seek to date her anymore, but turn your attention to finding someone else with whom your match is obviously better.

If, on the other hand, you're confident you would like to marry her, or at least to consider it seriously, then declare your interest on the fourth date. Stop short of proposing to her then, to be sure, or announcing that you know beyond all doubt you want to marry her. She may take such an extreme display of interest as abrupt or unreliable, giving your brief acquaintance. Speak in terms, rather, of seriously considering the option of marriage together. Explain to her that you're very impressed with her, and would like to think of further dating as a chance to explore the possibility of marrying. Would she be interested?

If she responds that no, she doesn't want to consider marrying you, be gracious. Thank her for her honesty (and be grateful for it, for you've cleared the air on this relationship). But explain to her that you're eager enough to marry that it wouldn't be right from your standpoint to continue dating her, nor would it be kind for you to take up her time. For the sake of keeping your mission to marry on course, chart this one up to experience, leave this relationship behind, and focus on looking for someone new.

If she tells you she is open to the possibility of marrying you, and to further dating as a courting period, then the ice is thoroughly broken. You shouldn't have much difficulty talking about marriage from this point on.

Even if you're convinced early on that you want to marry her, you usually do best to wait at least three months before declaring so unreservedly. Assuming yours is an active dating relationship—you're seeing each other at least once a week and communicating several times between—then by about three months you cross a line where your judgment becomes more trustworthy, and a proposal of marriage has greater credibility to her.

If you continue to be uncertain, the question of how long to wait before finally deciding about the relationship is trickier. The dynamics of every relationship are different, not to mention how frequently you see each other. But if your dating relationship is anything close to active, and you're truly ready to leave singleness for marriage, then usually by six months you know each other well enough to decide responsibly about marrying. If you're still undecided, then you need to be very honest with yourself. What further information about this person or about your compatibility as a couple would it take for you to decide confidently? If you can identify specific things you still need to know, or specific experience you still need together (meeting either's family, for instance), then strive to gain that insight or experience as soon as you can.

At this point in your relationship, though, you may be surprised to find you can't clearly specify further information or experience that would make a decisive difference. What's holding you back, rather, is the desire to let your feelings settle more. Some further dating to allow this to happen may be justified. But if you're personally ready to get married, rarely should you let a dating relationship continue beyond a year without resolving whether to marry. It's simply unlikely you'll gain any critical new insight beyond this point, and inertia is such a powerful force in long-term dating relationships. In fact, within six months to a year of dating, you typically reach, much more quickly than you realize, a saturation point where you actually have too much information about each other rather than too little. It's "paralysis through analysis" time, where commitment alone will make a difference in your feelings.

I understand the other side to this. A deadline for deciding may compel you to choose unwisely to marry or prematurely to break up. You may decide to marry from pressure or a longing not to lose the other's companionship, when you would be better off not marrying. Or you may choose to break up when further dating would lead to a confident decision to marry. True, you cannot remove the element of risk in any decision to marry or break up. Risk is always involved, no matter your maturity, your relationship's longevity, or your confidence you're right—as a look at the experience of countless couples you know quickly shows. Marriage is for adults, and the decision to marry is the most adult of all decisions you'll ever make. It requires a healthy willingness to risk, remembering that the greatest rewards in life tend to come from choices we make with the greatest "fear and trembling."

And the greatest challenge to responsibly deciding about marriage comes from the fact that our psyches don't handle long-term indecision well. We tend to imagine that more insight and experience will allow us finally to decide confidently whether to marry someone. Yet most of us are so wired that the deepest and most healthy love we can feel for a romantic partner comes only after we've committed ourselves for life to this person. At that point— and when the match is right—our psyche kicks in and helps us in numerous ways to feel the confidence that so far has eluded us.

If you've dated for a reasonable period and are almost persuaded to marry, it's doubtful further dating will push you over the brink to confidence. Only the decision to marry will. If after a year of dating, you don't feel comfortable enough to take that leap of faith, then—as hard as it may be—give your partner her freedom, and take yours as well, to allow you both to start your quest for marriage over. You'll still find you've benefited immensely from the relationship. What you've learned from it will make it easier now to find someone right for you, and to decide with less agony about marrying that person.

If you do find yourself indecisive in the six-month-to-one-year period, I strongly recommend finding a confidant—a wise, trusted friend, or a professional counselor—who can help you sort things through. Draw on this person's assistance as much as necessary, to work through your feelings and to determine whether your lack of resolution is due to unreasonable expectations or fears, or the result of legitimate concerns. As I've stressed throughout this book, such a person's help can be invaluable both in seeking someone to marry and in the decision itself, and especially at this critical juncture.

From the woman's perspective. I've been looking first at initiating talk and choices related to marriage from a man's standpoint, since men in America are most often expected to propose, and many feel it's their obligation to initiate serious discussion. Yet the dynamics of relationships vary greatly. Every relationship is different, as is every man and woman in a relationship. In many cases it's more appropriate, and simply works better, for the woman to initiate marriage talk some or most of the time. This makes sense for you as a woman if you're comfortable doing it, and especially if your partner is shyer or more introverted than you. It can make sense too if the man, even though wanting to marry you, is inherently anxious about committing to marriage. You may be in a better position emotionally to direct the discussion. While, yes, there's risk, he may appreciate the pull out of his inertia.

I advise you to follow the same time frames I've recommended for a man in deciding your own commitment to the relationship. Resolve by the fourth date if you want to consider this man for marriage, and only continue forward with the relationship if you do. Then resolve within three to six months, if you possibly can, whether you do want to marry him—but don't stay in the relationship beyond a year if you remain uncertain, or if he can't decide about marrying you.

It may work best for you also to be the one who initiates discussion about these transitions. It's fully appropriate on the first date—in fact recommended if he doesn't do it—to ask him if he wants to get married or stay single. Few men who have asked you out in the first place will be offended or think you abrupt to raise this question, and his response should allow you naturally to share your own thoughts. Keep the discussion academic on the first date, if you can—that is, limited to your views about getting married in general, but not to your relationship specifically.

If your relationship has passed the third month, you've been dating actively, and you know you would like to marry him, it's also totally appropriate for you to initiate discussion about the two of you marrying. But you have greater freedom to do this with the interrogative—that is, to start by asking his feelings. Normally, he would be judged inconsiderate to first ask your feelings before declaring his. You, though, are on comfortable ground to take this tactic, and also to be a bit indirect. For instance, "John, do you think you and I could do well as a married couple?" If you prefer he raises it first, give him up to six months to do it. But if you're convinced you want to marry him, I strongly recommend that by then you do something inquisitive like this to stimulate the discussion.

If he does respond that he wants to marry you, then tell him you would greatly appreciate a formal proposal, and that you would like him to surprise you with it. That will allow him to take what will be likely be the most memorable and symbolic point of initiative in your courtship. Yet you're on good ground to get the discussion going first, if the dynamics of your relationship recommend it.

Proposing formally. Which brings us to a distinction that may be obvious to you, but not necessarily. Most couples today who decide to marry do so in two stages—first through informal discussion, then through a more formal proposal. What I've been talking about so far is the informal (or less formal) part of this process, where you both make clear that you want to marry each other. This discussion may logically take place on a date in a formal setting (a fine restaurant), but may just as well occur anywhere—at one of your homes, on a walk, while you're traveling together. And either of you may feel fully comfortable initiating it.

It's from the assurance of this discussion that a formal proposal usually happens later, and most often is initiated by the man (though I'll look at an exception in the next chapter). Then, the setting by definition should be formal and ceremonial: a candlelight dinner, a canoe ride at sunset, a harbor cruise. Here the man may present an engagement ring, and the occasion itself is a celebration of your decision to marry.

Of course, there's nothing in the constitution saying a man can't pop the question initially through such a formal proposal, and some prefer to do it that way. It's certainly more dramatic and ceremonial. It also can be high risk, depending on how well you, the man, know your partner. Normally, I wouldn't recommend making a formal proposal your first occasion of discussing marriage (and especially not if you're presenting a ring), unless you like to live dangerously, or have compelling reason to believe she'll joyfully accept.

In most cases, it simply isn't necessary to begin this way. The woman may experience just as much surprise and jubilation if you first bring up marrying informally, then in a moment of high drama

at a five-star restaurant. In fact, she may prefer this two-stage approach, for it may allow her a greater sense of participating in the
decision and not feeling pressured into it. Imagine her awkwardness if she wasn't certain about marrying you, yet you presented
her a ring during an expensive meal, with obviously high expectations.

When in doubt, I strongly recommend you begin with the less
formal discussion. You'll not likely go wrong doing so, and you'll
probably show greater sensitivity to her needs by starting there.

Courting an Old or Current Friend

If you're starting a dating relationship from scratch with a new, or
fairly new, acquaintance, the rules for serious talk I've suggested
so far normally make sense. You have permission—usually a mandate—to wait a while before broaching discussion about your relationship and the possibility of marrying. At the same time, if you're
on a serious mission to find someone to marry, you don't want to
wait too long before talking seriously and resolving the relationship's
direction. The key is striking a balance; if you come on too strong
at first, you may convey insincerity to the other or even frighten her
away.

But what if you're looking up an old friend or lover, with the
hope of reviving your relationship and considering marriage? Or
what if you're hoping to convert a current friendship with an
opposite-sex friend to a courtship? In these cases (and, again, to
say the obvious), the dynamics are different from the situation we've
been looking at so far, for here you're building on a foundation of
established friendship and, in some cases, intimate understanding
of each other. And so launching serious talk about marriage may
need a different approach.

Serious marriage talk with an old or current friend may begin
spontaneously. Because of the bond and energy already there between you, such natural discussion is more likely to ignite than with
a new acquaintance. You may suddenly find that the God who has

been changing your heart has been changing your friend's as well, and that talk about marrying occurs even at an unlikely time, like when riding the subway home from work or at a church social. Be open and hopeful about this happening.

At the same time, you may have to take strategic initiative to spark such serious talk, even when a friendship is ripe for a new direction. The nature of your relationship with your opposite-sex friend, of course, may be at any of a variety of levels. If it's an old acquaintance, it may be someone you knew only as a friend, or someone you had once dated seriously, or someone between these extremes (the friendship had romantic overtones but you never dated seriously). If it's a current friendship, it may be someone you've known casually for some time but with whom you've never spent much time. Or it may be a hang friend with whom you've logged so much time, and shared so many romantic hints, that you feel almost married. Or it may be someone between these extremes. Yet all of these situations are similar in that you're hoping to convert a dormant friendship or a current one to a courtship.

And here you have two general approaches to consider:

Let's talk. One option is for the two of you to get together specifically for a serious talk. Ask your friend if he or she will meet with you to talk about a matter that's important to you personally. While you may do this on a date *per se*—at a nice restaurant, for instance—you can also choose any setting that's natural for you—a park bench, a stroll in the woods, a visit to either of your homes. And either of you can feel comfortable initiating this time.

When you meet, explain to your friend that your perspective on both life and your relationship has been changing. You've found yourself growing more serious about wanting to be married. And you've also been thinking long and hard about the two of you, and wondering if in fact you would be well matched for marriage. Mention some redeeming qualities of your friend that have stirred your interest. And ask her if she would be open to a courting/dating relationship, where you seriously consider together the possibility of marrying.

If you're already confident you would like to marry her, and know her well enough to trust that conviction, then you may want to tell her so. But if you believe telling her would be too abrupt and might overwhelm her—and especially if it's an old friend whom you haven't seen in a while—then keep it to suggesting you two *consider* marriage for now. Allow her a fair opportunity to grow into her own conviction about your relationship before declaring yours more unreservedly.

And if you personally are just at the consideration stage, then don't promise more than you can deliver. Explain that you are seriously wondering if you two might have a future, and would greatly appreciate a generous opportunity to weigh this hope together through a committed dating relationship.

If she replies that she isn't interested in considering marriage or in a serious relationship with you, then ask her if her no is final. Would she be willing to think about it for a while? And is it okay to ask her again? If she tells you her decision is final, then—again, out of respect for her and stewardship of your time—accept her no as permanent. After this one meeting, don't immerse yourself in a mission to change her mind. Leave this one in God's hands, and trust that if any mind changing is to happen, he is better able to do it without your help. Indeed, the strategy of the strategic retreat sometimes does work, so don't give up all hope she might change her mind. But don't park your life there either; turn your attention now to finding someone else.

If she asks for some time to consider it all, then maintain light contact with her for a while—occasional e-mail, perhaps, or whatever hang time customary for you. If she doesn't bring the matter up again on her own, wait six weeks and then ask her again. If she says she would still like more time, allow another six weeks and then bring it up again. If she still isn't certain, then I recommend the three-strikes rule now. Since she has given an ambivalent response these three times, the risk is strong you'll get bogged down in an inert situation with her. Explain that out of respect for her and managing your time responsibly, you need to move on now to find someone more interested in getting serious with you.

If realizing she'll lose this opportunity with you moves her to ask earnestly for more time, with a promise to try to make up her mind soon, then allow another six-week period. Otherwise, you should let her go.

If she does agree to a courting relationship, then follow the time limits I've already suggested for deciding your relationship's direction. Think of these as maximum deadlines, though. You two may be able to decide more quickly about marrying than if you were new acquaintances, since you already know each other, and possibly well. In any case, you each should try to resolve the question within six months of serious dating. And if after a year, one or both of you still can't decide, you should—out of respect to you both—choose to move on.

Ask her out. There's a second approach you can take to try to convert an old or current friendship to a courting relationship. Rather than ask if you can talk, simply ask her for a date. If she accepts, that's a hopeful initial sign, and from there seek to launch a dating relationship. Follow my guidelines for when to broach serious topics, but again as maximum periods for doing so, for the friendship history you already share may help accelerate discussion about marriage.

Asking someone for a date is symbolic. If you ask out an old friend whom you haven't seen for a while, or a current hang friend, you're conveying potential romantic interest in this person without saying so overtly. Your friend's accepting the date may also convey such interest in you. You're then able to test the waters a bit before talking seriously, and let your confidence grow. If she accepts a second date with you, and then a third, you have a greater indication she may be open to getting serious.

Whether you should seek to launch a courting relationship with this friend through talking first or dating first is a judgment call.

You'll simply need to trust your instincts as to which approach best suits this friendship. As always, if you have someone trusted whom you can consult with about it, you may find their advice invaluable.

If you're a woman hoping to convert a friendship with a man to a serious relationship, you can certainly feel comfortable asking him on a single date without fearing he'll think you brazen. Your friendship history with him gives you permission to initiate a date, as a way of "dropping the handkerchief." He'll not likely think you brazen, and indeed may welcome your initiative. In the best case, your significant hint of liking him will ignite his own initiative, and he'll ask you out in return, sparking an ongoing dating relationship. If he doesn't pick up the ball at this point, yet still shows interest in you, it raises the question of what further initiative you should take. We'll explore this and other questions related to your taking initiative as a woman in the next chapter.

Sixteen

* * * * * * * * * *

Taking Your Best Iniative as a Woman

FRANK AND LINDA HAVE A SECRET. THEY'VE ONLY SHARED it with a few trusted friends during their 20 years of happy marriage. It's not that they feel ashamed about it—quite the contrary. But they do fear that some in their church wouldn't understand.

The secret is that Linda proposed to Frank.

Well, at least, sort of.

"Linda was the first to suggest getting together," Frank admits. "And I'm so glad she did. I was so uneasy around the opposite sex that I blushed just seeing a woman's picture. After several awkward conversations at church, she asked if I'd come to her home one Sunday afternoon to watch a football game."

"I did pick up the reins from there," he points out. "Her making that first move did wonders for my courage, and I began to call her frequently. But at several points when I got scared and stopped phoning, Linda had to jumpstart our relationship. She got me talking again, and helped me realize that I really did want it to continue.

"Finally, she had the courage to say what I hadn't been able to bring myself to say. She told me she would like to spend the rest of her life with me. I'll tell you, I sure picked up the ball after that. A week later, I took her to a classy restaurant and formally proposed as were eating the main course. I thought she'd get us kicked out for the shouts of joy that came out of her mouth! It was just wonderful. But I really have my doubts I could have reached this point with a less assertive woman than Linda. I'm eternally grateful for her taking the initiative she did."

Challenging the Custom

Like many readers, you may not find Linda's initiative at all radical or audacious—in fact, it may make perfect sense. You may indeed feel she would have been justified taking much stronger initiative, without ever needing to apologize to anyone. Yet if you're a Christian, as many of my readers are, you may wonder if Linda overdid it, even with this fairly innocent level of assertiveness. While God seems clearly to have blessed their relationship, is it perhaps in spite of Linda's initiative rather than because of it?

The question of a woman's initiative in relationships is much more than an academic one for many Christians. Many Christian women, faced with the reticence of so many Christian men, would love to feel free to take the sort of basic initiative that Linda did, if not more. And many, frankly, would greatly improve their prospects if they did.

Yet Christian women face a serous constraint here. Traditional Christian thinking, with its emphasis on male headship, has frowned upon women playing anything but a quiescent role in relationships. In many Christian circles, it's regarded as out of place for a woman to take such basic steps as phoning a man for a date or even suggesting in a casual way that they get together. Her role is to wait passively and prayerfully and to leave it to the man to do the pursuing. There has been some rethinking of this point among Christians in recent years. Internet dating services have also shaken the rafters a bit, helping many Christian women feel more comfortable taking certain initiative, at least online. Yet the traditional outlook remains strong and is often taught and counseled, leaving many Christian women conflicted about what initiative, if any, is appropriate for them to take.

You may remember I began this book with the story of a Christian woman in her mid-forties who longed to be married, but felt her hands were tied when it came to initiating opportunities with men. She was no wallflower, but a publicist for the White House and a vivacious, attractive woman. Many of her Christian female friends felt similarly, even though the church they attend is a large, mainline, metropolitan one. In fact, the teaching and counseling on a woman's role in relationships in many churches tends to be restrictive, and discourages women from taking initiative with men.

Our secular culture, too, doesn't make it easy for women in this respect, and at best sends them mixed signals. While the feminist movement has proclaimed emphatically that a woman should feel free to play any role she wants in a relationship, strong currents of traditional thinking still exist throughout our society. Depending upon where you grew up, and the attitude of your family and friends, you may have been strongly admonished to leave the initiating to the man. It's fair to say that the belief a woman should wait demurely for her prince to come still prevails in more segments of our culture than not.

Many assume that these attitudes of our Christian and secular cultures originate in Scripture. The Bible, though, when carefully examined on the point, is found to present a different and much more liberating perspective. While it has plenty to say about women (as well as men) being respectful and not pushy in relationships, it says nothing against a woman's being the initiator at important stages of a relationship. To the contrary, in the most elaborate description of a courtship in the Bible—that of Ruth and Boaz in the book of Ruth—it is Ruth who takes the initiative to let Boaz know she is open marrying him (Ruth 3). While she isn't at all brazen, neither is she squeamish about putting herself in a position where Boaz will have no doubt about her hopes.

Nowhere else does Scripture forbid a woman from taking the initiative to begin a serious relationship, or from taking the lead to talk about the relationship's direction or marriage itself. As a matter of principle, she should certainly feel the same freedom at these points that a man does. Our uneasiness with this perspective, I'm convinced, springs from cultural conditioning and not from sound biblical understanding. Here I agree heartily with Christian sociologist Herbert J. Miles, who insists that a single Christian woman "has a right to take the initiative by correspondence, telephone, or personal contact to meet and become acquainted with any person she is interested in knowing better."[17]

Miles not only observes that Christian women, as all women, should have this right, but notes distinct advantages that come from exercising it:

> There are several benefits when women take the initiative. It could mean an end to some long, lonely evenings and weekends. Her initiative would give her a wider selection. It could mean more marriages. Since women tend to look more deeply than just physical attractiveness, they are more likely to find a more compatible mate. Female initiative would tend to produce better marriages. The courtship role is key to planning marriage and life. Nature and society have thrust upon women the responsibility of child-bearing and much of the responsibility of the home. Surely the woman should have the right to choose a life companion who would be meaningful to her across the years.[18]

There's a further reason why it's often good for a woman to take initiative. More often than not, she's more comfortable socially than the man, who may even be considerably shy. It only makes sense in these cases for her to be the first one who opens up. Apart from her initiative, the relationship may never get off the ground. Frank and

Linda's is a classic case in point.

Exercising Discretion

The bottom line is that a woman should feel free to take whatever initiative will benefit her in getting to know a man or in furthering a relationship, and a Christian woman is free to take the same initiative as any other. How, then, do you determine what initiative will work best with a given man? Most men won't be offended if you take *some* initiative, though some may be if you take too much. Here you simply have to pray, trust your instincts and make a judgment call. If the man seems shy, chances are he'll greatly appreciate your being straightforward about getting together. I can testify that, as a shy single, I was grateful and never offended when on several occasions women took such initiative with me.

There are many low-key approaches you can take. If the man in whom you're interested attends church with you, for instance, you might suggest having lunch together following the morning service, or ice cream after an evening meeting. Keeping the situation easygoing and low-budget also keeps the question of who should pay from becoming a big issue. Be ready to pay for both of you or for yourself, but if he offers and seems earnest, allow him to cover it.

You might try a similar approach if you and he are in a class together, attend the same club or association, are coworkers, or share some other activity. Suggest you have coffee, dessert, or a meal following the event or day at work, and at a convenient place. Such a get-together is less formal than a date, since it's spontaneous and a natural transition from what you're doing together, and it isn't something you prepare for and anticipate. Even though low-key and relatively safe (you don't lose much face if he declines or fails to start initiating on his own), your merely suggesting it signals your potential interest in him. If he is likewise attracted to you, this informal time—or just your asking, even if he's not available— may be all he needs to boost his confidence to pursue you, and he may start taking significant initiative after that.

A bolder approach is to ask him on an actual date. As I noted in the last chapter, this can be an ideal move if you want to try to convert a significant friendship to a serious relationship. Few long-time male friends will be offended if you ask them out—indeed, most will be flattered. And, of course, it's highly appropriate for you just to ask an old or current friend if you two can meet to talk. Asking for the talk or a date are both justified approaches in this case where you hope to change the nature of your friendship.

It's a bit riskier to ask out a man you don't know well. Yet if you don't share an activity with him that provides the chance to suggest a spontaneous, casual get-together, then asking him on a date may be wise—especially if you've already hinted interest in him and he hasn't responded. In this case, nothing ventured, nothing gained. And if he's shy, or just hasn't picked up your hints, your asking him out may give him just the signal he needs to begin pursuing you, and may boost his confidence enough to do so.

If he turns you down, well . . . I recommended a three-strikes rule for a man asking out a woman. For a woman asking out a man, though, two strikes is much wiser to heed. If he turns you down courteously and reluctantly (clearly explains why he's unavailable), and expresses hope you'll ask him again, then wait a week or two (longer if you wish) and give him another chance.

But if he declines again for any reason—and no matter how earnestly he asks you to try again—let it go now, and leave it to him to take the next initiative. By asking him out twice, you've declared your interest in him strongly enough. Since he has more permission socially to ask you out—and it's the courteous, gentlemanly thing for him to do now if he's attracted to you—you should leave it to him to do that, if he's so inclined. His failure to do so indicates he's not attracted to you enough to merit your pursuing him further. You're also likely to come off as pushy if you ask him a third time when he hasn't reciprocated. While it may be justified with an extremely shy man, a third effort isn't likely to be taken well by most men.

I recommend the two-strikes rule also when asking a man to do something casual following a mutual activity. A fellow church member, for instance, may take your invitation to have lunch following a service as just pleasant friendliness on your part. But trying a second time, more strongly indicates your interest in him. The gentlemanly response at this point is for him to return the favor. If he doesn't, asking him a third time may seem pushy. Again, it may be appropriate with an extremely shy man—you'll need to trust your instincts then—but not with most men, who by now will be adequately prompted to take some initiative. (An exception is if you're asking him to join a group going out for lunch; then you can feel free to hound him again from time to time. But not when you're suggesting just the two of you do something together.)

If the relationship you try to spark picks up steam, and the man begins asking you out, you of course can continue initiating some dates yourself as well. A sharing of initiative takes place in most healthy relationships, and yours will likely begin to define its own pace. You also may find it necessary or advisable to take initiative at certain transition or crisis points. Again, Frank and Linda's relationship is a typical example. Linda needed to draw Frank out several times when he was ready to put things on the shelf. In these instances, she understood his feelings better than he did, and her sensitive initiative saved the relationship. And if she hadn't finally suggested the idea of marrying, she might still be waiting for Frank to pop the question.

You should always feel very free to be the one who initiates serious discussion about marriage, especially if you're more naturally comfortable doing so. If he does agree to marry you, you should feel equally free telling him you would appreciate a formal proposal—if that's important to you (it is to most women)—and for him to surprise you with it. While there's nothing in the Bible or the constitution requiring a man to propose formally, nor ruling out a woman's doing it, the tradition of the man ceremonially proposing is deeply ingrained in ours and most cultures. And a man who truly wants to marry you will likely comply happily if you ask him to.

You probably won't need to make this request of him, as most men will instinctively understand the importance of proposing formally. But if you're not certain he will, then ask him what he thinks of the idea of a formal proposal in general. If he indicates he doesn't think it's necessary or important, then now is the time to explain clearly to him that this formality is important *to you*.

Many Options

Whether or not you choose to take serious initiative to get a relationship going, you always have many less assertive options that can be highly effective. If the man whom you wish to know is fairly comfortable socially, then it may make sense to allow him a fair opportunity to make the first move. You can still be clear in letting him know you would like to get to know him better, and casual suggestions may be all that are necessary. Statements like, "I really enjoy talking with you," or, "I hope I'll have more opportunity to see you," may give him all the cuing he needs. If after a month or two he hasn't followed through, then you're certainly in order to suggest getting together for lunch or a casual time, or even to initiate a date. Pray and use your best discretion.

And if you're wrestling with your freedom as a Christian woman to take initiative with men, remember that biblically you have the right to do whatever is helpful to launch a relationship or help it along. And if you have this right, then this just might be where taking a step in faith will open you more fully to God's provision. Be open to this possibility, especially if things are at a standstill in your dating life and have been for some time.

And remember also what may not seem so obvious: Most men, even the most confident socially, are flattered by a certain level of initiative from you. And those who are shy or socially inexperienced may be relieved and truly grateful for it. In some instances, it truly is a case of nothing ventured, nothing gained, and makes the difference between a relationship's prospering or failing to ignite.

Part Four

* * * * * * * * * *

Staying the Course

Seventeen

* * * * * * * * * *

Making Every Day Count

DURING THE CALIFORNIA GOLD RUSH, A PROSPECTOR named R. U. Darby helped his uncle mine a vein of gold that the latter had discovered. It appeared at first that they had a prosperous find. Yet the vein soon disappeared, and Darby and his uncle searched frantically for the spot where it continued. Finally, they concluded their prospects were hopeless and sold their equipment to a junk dealer.

The junk dealer consulted an engineer, and then began mining the shaft again. He quickly discovered the elusive vein and a supply of gold worth millions of dollars—just three feet from where Darby and his uncle had stopped digging.[19]

The story brings to mind how our important battles in life are often won by simple persistence. It reminds us equally that we can give up on a goal too easily, and are sometimes much closer to hitting our mark than we realize.

When we look at what made the accomplishments of notable individuals possible, we usually find persistence that went beyond the ordinary. Thomas Edison invented the incandescent light bulb only after thousands of failed attempts. He remarked, "The trouble with other inventors is that they try a few things and quit. I never quit until I get what I want."

We might imagine that underlying most notable accomplishments is dogged, backbreaking effort. More typically, though, the secret lies in *consistent* effort. Victory comes to those who stay with a dream long enough to reach it. In so many cases, this patient plodding overrides serious limitations in ability, education, or resources. Persistence plays this compensating role in endless areas of human achievement. Research shows, for instance, that drilling companies that discover the most oil are not the ones with the best equipment or the most talented personnel—but those that dig the most wells.

While it may seem only obvious that persistence makes every difference in many of our accomplishments, we're less inclined to think of it as important in seeking marriage. But as we've stressed time and again throughout this book, persistence is essential if most of us are to achieve this goal. This delightful story of a junk dealer's sudden good fortune finding gold provides an excellent basis to make some further points about what persistence means for those of us seeking the gold in relationships—the prize of a wonderful marriage—and what the implications are for how we think and spend our time. And this will allow me to end this book with some further strains of hope—that yes, you can do it!—as well as some admonition to stay the course and continue doing those things necessary to succeed.

The story has four implications that can keep your heart encouraged and your life productive as you seek that person who is right for you. Please don't close this book without considering each of these points carefully.

1. Marriage for you may be just "around the corner." The first point is that you may be closer—even much closer—to realizing your dream of finding someone to marry than you realize. Here's what's most interesting about this particular goal: Most major life objectives we embrace are labor- and time-intensive to a degree we cannot greatly reduce. If you decide to pursue an academic degree, for instance, you may get a break here and there for life experience or past study. Yet you still have a mountain of clearly defined work to accomplish before receiving that cherished diploma, and there's no way to reach that summit other than fully climbing to it.

This same dynamic applies to career goals. You may get certain breaks. Yet you'll most likely have to work many years and meet many challenges before achieving the position you most want. Likewise with financial goals. Most of us, with rare exceptions, will see our nest egg grow substantially only with years of diligent work and careful investing. And of course, we can't shortcut the development of a critical skill. One important study found that 10,000 hours is typically required to gain mastery of a significant talent.

And so on with most major goals. Yet the goal of finding someone to marry—the most intense dream most of us ever harbor—works differently. Yes, it will probably take work and time and plenty of patience. Yet at any point—literally, on any day—we may suddenly get a breakthrough and achieve our heart's desire. That vein of gold we suspected was just a fantasy, or so out of reach not to merit our effort, is suddenly in our sight.

And so the goal of finding someone to marry is really more akin to the ancient art of prospecting than to most life goals we pursue today. As I've stressed throughout this book, hope is vital to your success in finding a mate, because it makes you more alert to good opportunities and gives you the heart to pursue them. Having hope also makes you more attractive as a person. The lack of hope that you'll find someone to marry is as sure to repel certain prospects as strong hope is likely to attract them.

I urge you to keep R.U. Darby's story in mind constantly, as a metaphor to this major goal you've taken on, and take a moment each day to remind yourself that the golden opportunity you seek may indeed be just around the corner. This isn't blind positive thinking—which I don't recommend and is counterproductive. If you're at least into your twenties and ready for marriage, then envisioning it as around the corner is a reasonable hope that can only contribute to your success.

2. You most likely still have some work to do that you can't shortcut. Hope will contribute to your success *if* it inspires you to be active, not passive. The junk dealer was no naive positive thinker, imagining hope alone would make it so. He knew he still had work to do, which he set about doing carefully and diligently. It was that *effort*, ultimately, that brought him victory. Yet he made this effort because he believed success was around the corner.

The around-the-corner principle will inspire you to see the best possible actions you can personally take toward your goal of marriage, and will stimulate you to take them. Consider this adventure fantasy for a moment: What if God were to send an angel to you, who stands before you and announces that you will find the love of your life for sure in one month—*providing* you take four strategic steps toward that goal in the meantime. These steps can be any you wish, but should be among what you believe the best available to you right now. Of course, your mind would immediately go into overdrive and serve you up with options you would pursue as quickly as possible.

What would these particular steps be for you personally? Devoting a day to the inventorying process I've recommended? Throwing caution to the winds and looking up an old friend? Pushing beyond shyness and phoning that friend at the gym? Attending the church singles class for the who-knows-what-teenth time? Going to the dance at the Legion Hall? Setting up a meeting with an online acquaintance? Taking a ski trip with a singles group? Attending their regular meeting, and making the effort to meet as many new people as you can?

Of course, God isn't going to send you the sixteen-foot angel, nor a five-foot one. But the same mind that you can imagine working so well for you under that circumstance will function just as effectively if you let hope inspire you as it should. Give enough time each day to nurturing the hope your soul mate will soon cross your path, to the point this hope truly cheers you. Also, assume as a matter of principle that you'll need to take as many as four significant steps to cross the barrier between you and this person. Decide what your best options are, and then set about doing them. If after taking these steps the prize still eludes you, then start the process over. God, again, has made you remarkably resilient. The hope we're speaking of can reignite at any time and continue to be this productive force for you.

But stay active, and mine your opportunities as best as you can. Picture that mine the junk dealer bought, and remember that just three feet of earth remained between the open space and the vein of gold yet undiscovered. And consider that no matter how brazenly optimistic this man was, no matter how strongly convinced he would succeed, digging away that remaining dirt was essential to gaining his prize. By the same token, no matter how pessimistic the former owner was, no matter how certain he would fail, had he removed that same dirt he would have succeeded equally. Bring this lesson to mind often, and let it be an admonition—whether you're feeling hopeful or discouraged—to *do something,* and to take advantage of your next best opportunity. Staying proactive like this will contribute the most to your success, and staying in motion will regenerate your hope as well.

3. Get the best coaching you can. The third lesson this story teaches us—or, in our case reminds us of—is the importance of getting expert counsel. The junk dealer did something Darby's uncle apparently didn't: he sought advice from a mining engineer. The engineer's counsel gave this new owner reasonable hope for success, as well as an understanding of how to move forward. Why Darby's uncle didn't seek such counsel we can only speculate. He may have thought it unnecessary, or may have been too prideful to solicit it. That mistake cost him a great fortune.

No matter what endeavor we take on, the right advice from

someone more experienced and knowledgeable so often makes the difference between our success and failure. I've stressed the importance of counsel in our search for marriage in this book, but this mining story provides the chance to preach it once again. Regardless of how fine a specimen of humanity any of us is, nor how much we have to offer in marriage, we have blind spots. We may be doing certain things that, unknown to us, are preventing our success. Yes, romantic chemistry is mysterious, and each of us, no matter how gifted with the opposite sex, will experience some rejection in our effort to date and launch relationships. But if you're failing repeatedly, or in similar ways, this may indicate you're shooting yourself in the foot in certain ways you're not recognizing.

Others typically see our blind spots much more readily and clearly than we do. If you have a trusted, insightful friend or pastor, who can counsel you wisely on relating to the opposite sex, avail yourself of this person's help to the fullest extent possible. Reread chapter 12, if you need to, where I offer guidance on how to tactfully seek this assistance. Then swallow your pride as much as you need to and ask for it. The good news is that the around-the-corner principle often applies with blind spots too. That is, you may only need to make some small changes in how you relate to the other sex to improve your options. Still, making them may be essential, and may make a huge difference in your success. Get the best counsel you can—and follow it.

Seriously consider getting professional counseling as well. Counselors with relationship expertise abound throughout our country, and you'll find them almost anywhere you live. Also prevalent are "life coaches," whose specialty is helping you live successfully and meet major goals—and some specialize in relationship skills. Whatever the cost required for professional counseling, consider it an *educational* expense. You've surely invested a fortune already in education for your career. Making a reasonable investment in training for relationships is equally justified, and not an area where you should skimp. And think of that cost as likely involving some experimenting; you may need to pay for sessions with several counselors en route to finding one who is right for you. The right counselor, though, can do you a world of good, and help you every bit as much as the consulting engineer did that new mine owner. Be diligent in seeking the very best professional help, if you need it, and willing to pay what it requires.

4. See your daily activities as opportunities to move closer to your goal of finding someone to marry. The fourth lesson is not as obvious as the first three, but it's just as important. The junk dealer became aware of the chance to purchase the mine as he was about his day-to-day business, doing what he did professionally. However lowly his job surely was, it brought him into contact with the opportunity of a lifetime. He was at the right place at the right time because he was *active,* and not just passively dreaming about striking gold, even though his activity involved a mundane line of work.

If I may expand this point just a bit: Everything you do in your day-to-day life can, in its own specific way, contribute toward your goal of finding someone to marry. You will also find it very helpful to think of the different activities of daily life as moving you toward this dream. Seeing them this way deepens your sense of purpose in many activities that otherwise may seem mundane. It also strengthens your hope that you're moving meaningfully toward your dream of marriage. And it makes you more alert to using your gift of time each day to take some beneficial steps toward that dream— it makes you a better steward of your time, in other words.

Daily activities help you toward your goal of marriage in two broad ways. Some keep you socially active, positioning you to meet someone or for others to notice you and help you. Other activities help you grow and develop qualities that better suit you for marriage, and that make you more attractive as a person—especially to someone who is right for you.

The around-the-corner principle applies here too. On any given day an activity—even one seemingly irrelevant to your marriage search—may suddenly bring you into contact with the person you're to marry, or open the door for you soon to meet this person. Or you may take a step of growth that, even though incremental, is a tipping point, suddenly changing the balance in your mix of personal qualities and making you ready to succeed in your quest for someone to marry.

Some of these opportunities are obvious. You have the chance to attend the church social or the office party, or to ask someone out whom you've recently met, or to ask a friend's help, or to pursue a contact online. Other opportunities are less obvious, yet may still help you enormously toward achieving your goal. Some of these abundant daily-life opportunities include—

• *Steps to improve your financial stability.* Financial struggles stress and break up more marriages than any other issue. Often the problem centers on the debt one or both partners bring into the marriage. As much as you might like to keep your finances separate in marriage, the debt you personally carry invariably becomes shared by both of you. Creditors who hound one of you will hound the other as well, and significant debt weighs down the marriage in many ways.

Most who are seeking someone to marry hope that person will be as debt-free as possible, financially responsible, and a significant contributor to the marriage's financial stability. No matter what wonderful qualities you may bring to a marriage, if you're burdened with debt unreasonable to your income, or have poor financial habits, you're likely to scare certain people away who would otherwise be attracted to you.

Make it your goal to be in good shape financially, and to contribute significantly to the financial health of your marriage, rather than be a drain on it. Apart from possibly a home mortgage you can afford, strive to be free of any debt. If debt-free isn't realistic for you in the foreseeable future, then at least aim not to be *burdened* by debt. Then see each day as an opportunity to work toward this goal. Any effort you make today to be frugal, to resist the unnecessary purchase, to save and invest wisely, to earn a living, to keep better records, to stay on top of debt and taxes, to eschew any unhealthy financial habits (gambling, lottery, unreasonable lending to friends), to attend a seminar or read an article or book on managing finances, is a step of preparation toward finding your ideal mate. *Think* of such steps this way. It will increase your motivation to take them and your joy in succeeding once you do!

• *Your job and steps toward career advancement.* Of course, nothing affects your financial well-being more greatly than your job and career. Yet what you do professionally affects your relationship life in many ways beyond the financial.

For one thing, your job broadens you in countless ways and makes you a more interesting person. Your job likely provides frequent interaction with people, strengthening your conversation skills. And through immersing you in its own way in human life, your work makes you more alert to issues and events affecting everyone. In addition, if the person you date, court, or marry shares your line of work, your specific job-related skills are a point of interest to him or her, providing meat for conversation and plenty of opportunity for mutual support.

Your work environment is typically the best stage life provides you for improving your social skills. Scarcely a workday passes without offering prime opportunities to better understand others and how to relate to them effectively. Every work experience you have of managing your anger, defusing conflict, encouraging someone who's discouraged, presenting an idea convincingly, or interacting supportively with a team, influences your personality positively, giving you skills helpful in dating and courting.

Our work also, as much as anything we do, affects our self-esteem. For better or worse, most of us base our identity substantially on our job and career. And so anything we do to improve our daily work experience or embrace meaningful career goals strengthens our self-esteem. This boost in confidence in turn helps us in relationships, freeing us to take a greater interest in the other and be supportive.

Of course, anything we do in life has the potential to boost our self-esteem. But because we spend such vast time at our job, its potential to strengthen or squash our self-confidence is greater than most other activities. And so thinking of it as a venue for building our self-esteem is a wise mentality, and one that lends greater purpose to our daily work experience.

Finally, and perhaps most obviously, your job can be a prime venue for meeting someone to marry, or for others to take notice of your need and help you. Countless people meet their spouse through their work or through social connections forged through it. Of course, not every job provides a fertile social climate. Even if yours doesn't, it still offers the other benefits we've mentioned. Yet even the most mundane job may still, on any given day, bring you into contact with someone special—suddenly and unexpectedly. So stay open continually to this hope, and to the other benefits daily work brings in your search for a mate.

• *Health, vitality, physical fitness.* Each day also brings with it the chance to do certain things to improve your physical well-being. None of us is a perfect physical specimen, to be sure. In relationships and marriage, each of us makes allowance for certain physical issues the other has. If you have a serious, permanent disability, don't despair; there are those who will be drawn to you in spite of it—or even because of it. It's your unique combination of qualities that makes the difference and makes you attractive to others.

The key is to manage this combination as best as you can, to the extent you have control. Steps you take to maintain and improve your physical condition will help you in relationships, and for obvious reasons: Greater vitality means more energy to devote to a relationship, and you're better able to meet your partner's needs. Your ability to give yourself sexually depends on your physical condition to an important extent, as does your ability to be helpful in other ways. And since the person you court and marry will likely hope you take fitness seriously, you'll be able to meet that expectation or exceed it.

Strive to see the many choices you face each day that affect your health and vitality as opportunities to improve your prospects in relationships. Seeing them this way will give you the strength to say no to that second dessert, or to the mindless TV show that keeps you from your workout. Carefully plan an exercise routine that's right for you and stick to it. Be moderate in what you eat and drink, and maintain good sleep habits. This discipline will come back to you with many benefits when the chance for romance strikes, and will boost your energy and confidence as you search for that special person.

• *Physical appearance.* Of course, your physical well-being includes not just your health and vitality but how you look as well. And (to say the all-too-obvious) your appearance is high on the list of factors that cause others to rate you as attractive or not. Here again, though, your need isn't for perfection but to realize your best potential. Most who are serious about getting married and have mature expectations aren't looking for a "hot" partner, but for one who cares about their appearance and strives to present themself well. They want someone who has good hygiene, and who maximizes the potential of their physical appearance. Especially, they want a partner who feels good about how they look. This confidence about your appearance is sexy in itself and covers a multitude of shortcomings.

We can become too obsessed with looks, unquestionably, and the media pressure on women, especially, to maintain every nuance of a celestial Hollywood image is tragic. However, some reasonable and balanced attention to looks is appropriate and necessary for those of us looking for a relationship. Maintaining good hygiene, good dental health, and good grooming is essential, and creative attention to dress can take you a long way. Again, apply the golden rule: devote the attention to grooming and dress you would wish of someone you're dating.

And think of each day as a blank canvass on which you have the chance to present yourself appealingly to others, and appropriately to your circumstances. See it too as an opportunity to take steps, incremental and sometime major, to maintain your attractiveness over time and (if appropriate) to improve it.

• *Growing, learning, enjoying life.* While some days provide more leisure time than others, each day brings opportunities to do things that are fun and interesting to you. Whomever you marry will probably have high on their wish list the desire for their mate be interesting. Indeed, the fear of boredom probably keeps more from marriage than any other concern.

Anything you do on any given day that's stimulating or adventuresome, and anything that happens which deepens you, contributes positively to your personality, making you more interesting and attractive to others. Pursuing a hobby or avocation, reading a novel or practical book, attending a movie or play, or doing something purely adventuresome, may not seem obviously helpful in your search for love. Yet it's growing you, restoring you, and giving you more to bring to the table in a relationship. Consider how much conversational value there is in a single compelling movie, when someone you're with has also seen it.

See your leisure time not just as an opportunity to tune the world out (though that's sometimes necessary), but as a chance to stoke your inquisitive and adventuresome side. Seek to do things that are stimulating to you, that broaden your interest in life. You'll not only give yourself a boost, but you'll add to your quota of interesting experiences, giving you more to contribute to conversation in relationships.

• *Improving relationship skills.* Beyond our job, each day provides abundant opportunities to hone our social skills. On any normal day, most of us come into contact with numerous people— from intentional rendezvous with friends and necessary interaction with coworkers, to incidental encounters with neighbors, club members, salespeople, shoppers, fellow commuters, tourists, etc. See each day as a magnificent laboratory to polish your ability with people.

And keep in mind three things. One is that good social skills aren't natural for most of us, but have to be learned and practiced, to the point they become a *habit*. Second, the social skills that work well for us in a romantic relationship aren't greatly different from those effective with people in general, but are just focused more intensely on this one person. Third, no skill helps you more in a love relationship than the ability to take a genuine *interest* in your partner. And this inclination is particularly unnatural for most of us, since we tend by default to focus more on ourselves than others.

So take advantage of the many opportunities each day brings to be outgoing, to focus on others and take an interest in their experiences and needs. Be as friendly, supportive and encouraging as you possibly can, and, when appropriate, inquisitive. If this effort seems less than genuine, I can only tell you that, to an important extent, you have to "fake it till you make it" with social skills. You may feel like you're playing a role at first. But we feel unnatural initially developing any skill, don't we? Who feels at all comfortable when first learning tennis, golf, or any demanding sport? It's by sticking with it and fighting through the unnaturalness that we eventually develop a serious athletic skill, music or artistic ability. It's no different with social skills; we have to endure the sense that we're playacting at first. But others' positive responses help us feel more comfortable, and with time, outgoing behavior becomes more authentic to us, and a habit.

Give your personality this chance to transform itself. Determined, daily practice of social skills will do more to help you in relationships than you can imagine.

Seek also to be a *student* of social and relationship skills. There are countless books available on relating to people, on navigating every nuance of relationships, on how fellow humans tick, on understanding the other sex, on achieving goals and dreams, on finding someone to marry. Articles appear constantly in the press and on

the Internet as well. You can't begin to read everything, not remotely.
But sometimes even a brief moment of reading is life-transforming,
for an author targets a blind spot of yours that's preventing your
success. Taking the author's insight to heart and putting it into action truly brings you around the corner, and suddenly you're more
successful in this perplexing relationship world.

Devoting even a few brief minutes each day to reading something helpful on relationships, psychology, or goal setting, will likely
make a big difference over time, and the Eureka moments will surely
come.

• *Domestic skills.* Because marriage means living together, it
involves endless domestic tasks. These are shared responsibilities,
fortunately, and neither of you has to be highly skilled at every one.
One of you may be much more talented at sewing and restoring
worn clothing, for instance, and the other at certain household re-
pairs. And you always have to outsource certain tasks. Neither of
you may be skilled enough at plumping to replace a leaky pipe, yet
there's no shame in hiring a professional for this and other difficult
maintenance needs.

Yet someone who considers marrying you will want to know at
minimum that you take the home seriously, aren't allergic to household chores, and have some domestic skills to bring to the marriage. They'll want to know especially that you don't have any
lifestyle habits that would make living with you unpleasant. If you
habitually keep a messy home, that's a red flag and may well be a
deal killer. This is a good place to begin. Daily attention to the simple
task of keeping your home tidy and attractive will remove a potential barrier between you and marriage, and position you to make a
good impression on someone you court. (If you happen to be a compulsive hoarder, hasten to get the best professional help you can.
Earnestly strive to overcome this destructive habit, as it will likely
kill a good relationship quickly.)

Since marriage involves frequent meal sharing, any ability with
food and cooking will benefit you in courting. Here again is a skill

area each day gives you opportunity to develop. See your ongoing need to eat as a constant chance to grow your talent with food. Invest in some cookbooks, study them earnestly, and read your local paper's food section. Experiment, try new recipes often, and persist with techniques until you have them down. The better you become at preparing food, the more you'll enjoy it—and your pleasure in itself will make you more attractive as a potential spouse.

Beyond cooking and meal prep, any ability you learn—and learn to love—that improves home living is likely to help you in your search for someone to marry. Skill in carpentry and remodeling is a wonderful gift to any marriage, as is a talent for home decorating. Your enthusiasm for transforming your living space into a functional, warm, inviting environment—and your ability to contribute to this goal in specific ways—will appeal to anyone who considers marrying you. Investing your leisure time in learning a domestic skill is a wise step toward finding a partner. Use this talent in your current home as best as you can, and let it demonstrate to someone you're courting what you can bring to a marriage.

• *Conquering bad habits and behavior.* Compulsive hoarding isn't the only bad habit that can wreck a marriage and scare away someone from marrying you. Any addictive problem will do it, as will any behavior that makes you annoying, difficult to live with or befriend. If you are a practicing alcoholic, druggie, compulsive eater, easily angered, or habitually unkind or abusive, I cannot urge you strongly enough to get the best professional help available for overcoming the problem, and the strongest support network you can find. Even if you succeed in persuading someone to marry you, the marriage won't work as long as this tendency controls your life. Your partner's patience will give out at some point and the marriage will collapse, and so the effort to court this person isn't worthwhile for either of you. Focus your energy for now on conquering the problem and freeing yourself from its stranglehold on your life.

Healing must begin with facing your problem honestly and profoundly, and in humility admitting your need for help. In that spirit, seek God's help and that of people who are in a position to assist you. Get professional counseling, medical help if you need it, and locate and faithfully attend a support group of like-minded folks struggling with this same issue.

See each day as a welcome opportunity to draw on God's help, to seek support from others, and—as often as necessary—to successfully resist whatever pull this inclination continues to have. Remember that your destructive behavior is a *habit*, and it became so precisely because it was repeated time and again and reinforced in countless unhealthy ways. Your daily effort to alter this pattern can, with time and patience, forge a new habit that's nothing short of a personal transformation. Make such radical change your goal, and see each step toward it as one toward your dream of marriage, as well as toward a better, richer life for you in every other way.

• *Strengthening your compassion.* Compassion is also a habit, which some people display more obviously than others, and it's one that makes or breaks a marriage. Marriage is at its core about caring for another person wholeheartedly till death do you part. Anyone worth your marrying will be more concerned about how selfless and compassionate you are than about how beautiful and sharp a human specimen you appear to be. They'll notice acutely how you treat others and how attentive you are to their own needs. Compassion ebbs and flows to some extent, to be sure, and none of us can be Mother Teresa at every moment. Your ability to do what's right regardless of how you feel is important, and will be noticed and appreciated by someone your court. Still, your ability to feel authentic compassion and show it often is vital too, and your partner will see your heart for what it is.

God has created us with the capacity to feel compassion toward others, and to feel it strongly. To an important extent, though, this ability must be nurtured to reinforce the feeling of compassion, to the point it becomes a powerful force within us. A day rarely passes without offering many opportunities to act kindly and to choose loving responses over selfish ones. Every time the caring response wins out, compassion becomes a more ingrained habit and more natural for us on the next occasion. Here, as always, a word of caution is needed. You don't want to become a rescuer—that is, someone whose ego must be stoked constantly through apparent heroic acts of kindness. Compassion needs to be exercised with the mind as well as the heart. You can't meet every need that presents itself, or you'll burn yourself out. Give yourself wisely, in light of how you believe God is leading you to prioritize your time.

With these boundaries in mind, you still have great opportunity for acts of kindness that help shape your character into a more caring, sensitive one. Spontaneous opportunities arise practically every day to help friends, family members, coworkers, church or association members, and sometimes strangers, with their needs and emergencies. And no matter where you live, many organizations offer you the chance to lend your help to those with serious and chronic needs. Volunteering at a shelter, soup kitchen, nursing home, or hospital, can do as much for you in its impact on your personality as it does for those you help.

Recognize each day as a chance to stretch your heart and nurture your compassion. As you harvest the unique opportunities the day presents, you'll transform more into an attractive potential spouse, and better prepare yourself to win someone's hand for marriage.

Eighteen

* * * * * * * * * *

Concluding Thoughts

ON THANKSGIVING AFTERNOON 2007, OUR FAMILY traveled to a friend's home for dinner, about an hour's drive away. We returned home around 9:00 p.m., and Nate, who was still living with us then, left to visit with a friend. Then, about 9:30, an explosion like a cannon blast shattered the peaceful evening, and, seconds later, our electricity went out. The power transformer just up the street had blown, and our home and neighborhood were now dark.

Knowing it could be hours till a maintenance crew came and restored normalcy, Evie went to bed. I wasn't at all tired, and wanted to stay up. But now I was by myself in a dark home, with no television or computer access. The night was unusually warm, though, and so our home was comfortable; and through the windows, moonlight and starlight beautifully illuminated the surroundings outside. Our rural, wooded setting, plus the stony quiet enforced by the power outage (no appliance noise, no lights humming, no TV in the background), lent the sense of being on retreat in some rustic place. Our all-too familiar living space was suddenly transformed and now stunningly enchanting. This was the occasion for inspiration, I knew, and I began pacing around our home, waiting for any that might come.

The direction our thoughts take during a meditative time is sometimes surprising, and always interesting. Mine quickly drifted to the quest of certain single friends for marriage. I pondered the dilemma of a woman I had recently counseled who longed to be married, but had suffered many disappointments and seemed to be sabotaging her efforts in ways she didn't recognize. From there I mused more broadly about others I knew who were similarly discouraged in their search for a life partner. Then I thought more globally of the epidemic loneliness so many endure today who, while taking a certain pleasure in modern singleness, would strongly prefer the bonds of marriage, if they could simply find the right person who loved them in return.

I also sensed, as strongly as I ever have, that so many who've concluded their chances of ever happily marrying are nil, in fact have excellent prospects of finding someone highly suitable. They do, *if* they will stay in motion toward their goal, keep socially active, modify their ideals and approach in certain ways, and, most important, not give up hope. This race is won by those who stay in it, but many decide to opt out unnecessarily. Understandably, though, for a single romantic disappointment can crush us, and persuade us that risking that pain again isn't worth it. Yet the God who created us made us astoundingly resilient. He is also, in the words of the book of Ruth, a "restorer of life" (Ruth 4:15 RSV). He has, for those of us who are open to them, grand new adventures that have a remarkable way of healing past wounds.

I had felt similar stirrings of heart about twenty years before, but then toward people who were already in good relationships yet uncertain about marrying. I had known and counseled so many in strong, solid relationships—deeply caring friendships with someone of the opposite sex—who were hesitant to marry out of fear their romantic ideals wouldn't be fully met. I began to see patterns—the same issues coming up again and again, and the same misunderstandings, and so many who were missing the treasure before their eyes. Their struggles inspired me to write *Should I Get Married?*. It was my effort to help those in fear of "settling" resolve whether to marry, and decide which ideals are worth holding onto and which are not.

The awakening I felt this Thanksgiving evening was eerily similar, though this time I hurt for those who yearn to be married but have no opportunity. This burst of emotion was, I'm sure, the culmination of decades of counseling and interacting with people looking for relationships, plus my own often bungling efforts with women when single. Writers like to think of "The Muse" speaking to them. I prefer to think that, in the exquisite silence of that night, God had the opportunity to get my ear, and most important, to stretch my heart. At one point, I was moved to tears, thinking of the hopelessness so many feel who dearly long to marry but see no feasible way. I was moved even more, though, by the conviction I had something to give them in the way of counsel and encouragement that can help them achieve their dream. By the time our lights flashed back on, around midnight, I felt I had been commissioned to write a book for singles on finding someone to marry.

When I say "commissioned," I knew that, at the least, I had come to grips with something I deeply wanted to do. At best, I felt God had graciously prompted me about how to spend my writing time for a while. In either case, I knew it was time to get about doing it, and I resolved to devote whatever time and effort necessary to write this book. While I wanted it to help Christians especially with the unique issues they face, I hoped it would be broad enough in its focus to benefit anyone sincerely seeking the opportunity to marry. Marriage, after all, is a gift of God's "common grace" to all people, and a means by which they discover his goodness and draw closer to him. To restrict the discussion solely to Christians would be to miss the point that God extends this particular kindness to everyone.

It's now mid-November 2010, almost exactly three years later, and I've nearly finished the book which that Thanksgiving epiphany inspired. As I'm putting the final touches on it, I'm profoundly aware it's far from perfect. People looking for someone to marry are at vastly different points in their journey, and no book can hope to address every issue, concern, or need a given reader may have. At the same time, I can assure you I've given it my very best effort. I've never lost the burning desire, born that Thanksgiving evening, to help those who want to marry find a path to their dream. And it's my fervent hope that what I have written has helped you, and will continue to, in three significant ways.

First, I hope you have a clearer picture in your mind now of the sort of person who would be right for you to marry, and, especially, that your friendship with this person has become a more essential consideration. While most of us give lip service to the importance of friendship in marriage, we typically underestimate—often greatly—just how central it is to our long-term happiness. Instead, we spin our wheels seeking relationships that meet romantic ideals that are unrealistic and incapable of delivering the happiness we imagine. Most sadly, romantic idealizing can slow our search for the right person, and keep us from recognizing a truly good opportunity before our eyes.

Most books and articles published on this topic, including most I've seen since starting this book, continue to tread the same time-worn theme: *Look for someone who perfectly matches your ideals and dreams. Don't settle!!! If you have any doubt you've found the right person, don't go ahead.* Yes, you shouldn't settle in your search for a spouse—I agree! But this principle helps only if your expectations are reasonable and healthy in the first place. Most of us, unfortunately, are not good judges of our long-term happiness, and so marrying happily almost always requires modifying our ideals in certain ways. If we're harboring the hope that our marriage will meet certain storybook romantic ideals, and provide endless sexual nirvana, then we're setting ourselves up for disappointment and failure. Moderate romantic and sexual attraction, when combined with strong friendship and compassion, provides the best mix for lasting marital happiness. Your expectations then lead to far less stress than when romance and sexual ecstasy are your primary hope in marrying. And because a supportive spirit reigns supreme between you, enduring romantic love and sexual joy actually have the greatest chance to blossom.

I strongly hope this book has nudged you more toward this thinking about choosing a partner for marriage. If so, then the best news is that your revised expectations will likely help you in your search for a spouse, and may simplify it considerably, since you're now open to possibilities you weren't before. Not a few find that the prize they've been seeking is in their own backyard, so to speak. A friend they've known for some time but overlooked as a romantic companion suddenly is the obvious answer to their need for a lifemate.

I've also filled this book with the best practical advice I could provide. My second hope is that you've found at least some of this counsel helpful, will apply it where appropriate, and, most important, are now inspired to take serious initiative in your search for someone to marry. Few of us realize this dream without making considerable effort, taking significant risk, and fighting through plenty of discouragement, futility, and other negative feelings. The mentality that works best for us in the process isn't greatly different from that of a good salesman, who focuses not on his past disappointments but his new opportunities. This quest is won by looking forward, and stalled by dwelling on the past.

Being proactive breaks you out of the analytical mode that slows your search for marriage, greatly increasing your chance of meeting new people and having real-life opportunities to consider. In the end, the person you marry will not be an abstraction, nor an Internet fantasy, but a flesh-and-blood human creature. He'll meet your ideals in certain ways, but not others. And she'll surprise you in certain ways—being different from your long-held conceptions of the perfect mate, but over time, proving much better suited to your most important needs. And you'll make the amazing discovery that God, after all, knew far better than you what would most make you happy in the long run.

But you'll only position yourself for this grand discovery by staying in motion, taking risks, and regarding the whole process as a grand adventure. If this book has encouraged you to be more socially active and to take steps that better prepare you for marriage, then, whatever its limitations, the effort to write it has been more than worthwhile for me.

Finally, and more than anything else, I've wanted this book to boost your hope that you can find someone wonderful to marry, and enter a happy, deeply supportive lifetime bond with this person. I've striven to put this message of hope on every page, and wanted you to find your hope buoyed constantly as you've worked your way through this book. In fact, if this study has done nothing more than strengthen your hope that you can succeed, then I'm happy to have written it. And it's been worth your while to read it, for hope is the greatest essential in this quest. It enables you to overcome disappointment and see new possibilities, and it prods you to stay active and continue doing those things that will make your dream possible.

Among the many messages of hope that permeate Scripture is that God is on our side as we seek someone to marry, and supports us in countless ways. That message is there in very beginning of the Bible, where God, seeing that it wasn't good for Adam to be alone, provided a wife for him by miraculous means (Gen 2:18-25). We find it again in the first miracle of Jesus, performed at a wedding feast. When the refreshment ran out, he transformed six twenty-gallon jugs of water into the finest wine, saving face for this new couple in front of their family and friends (Jn 2:1-11). God supported them, in other words, as they took this huge step to marry, just as he had in helping them find each other.

And we see it instances where individuals find marriage by taking initiative and keeping their life in motion. Abraham's servant finds Rebecca for Isaac by leaving Canaan and traveling to Hanan (Gen 24). Moses finds a mate by leaving his Egyptian home and traveling to Midian, where he heroically assists a group of sisters being harassed by shepherds at a well. That so impresses their father, Reuel, that Reuel gives him his daughter Zipporah for his wife (Ex 2:15-22). Ruth finds Boaz by leaving Moab, the city of her bereavement, and returning to her original home of Bethlehem (Ruth 1-4).

And we find it, directly and indirectly, in so many promises of Scripture that speak of God's healing, restoration, and compensation in our lives (while we've looked at a couple of these before, please take heart from them again here at the end of our study):

The LORD builds up Jerusalem; he gathers the outcasts of Israel. He heals the brokenhearted and binds up their wounds (Ps 147:2-3).

A father to the fatherless, a defender of widows, is God in his holy dwelling. God sets the lonely in families (Ps 68:5-6).

He gives the barren woman a home, making her the joyous mother of children (Ps 113:9 RSV).

Instead of their shame my people will receive a double portion, and instead of disgrace they will rejoice in their inheritance; and so they will inherit a double portion in their land (Is 61:7).

Return to your fortress, O prisoners of hope; even now I announce that I will restore twice as much to you (Zech 9:12).

The LORD upholds all who are falling, and raises up all who are bowed down (Ps 145:14 RSV).

Finally, this message of hope is there in the obvious optimism of Paul, when he advises his Corinthian readers, "each man should have his own wife, and each woman her own husband" (1 Cor. 7:2). Paul is actually speaking more emphatically than this English translation implies, for in the Greek his statement is a *command*: "Let each man have his own wife, and let each woman have her own husband." What's most interesting is that Paul simply assumes the members of this small church, perhaps around 500 people, with limited options for travel, can find someone suitable to marry— and quite possibly within this congregation itself.

I've felt this same optimism for you, my reader-friend, throughout this book as I've written it. I hope this confidence has been strongly evident at every point, and has given you encouragement and fresh heart to stay devoted to your goal of finding a partner for marriage. May God bless you richly as you search for that person right for you, and I hope a day very soon brings the answer to your dream!

Notes

[1]Nita Tucker with Debra Feinstein, *Beyond Cinderella: How to Find and Marry the Man You Want* (New York: St. Martin's Press, 1987), p. 57.

[2]Daniel Gilbert, *Stumbling on Happiness* (New York: Vintage Books, 2007), pp. 3, 4, 17.

[3]Susan Page, *If I'm So Wonderful, Why Am I Still Single? Ten Strategies that Will Change Your Love Life Forever* (New York: Three Rivers Press, 2002), pp. 16-36.

[4]*Ibid.*, p. 21.

[5]*Ibid.*, p. 22.

[6]*Ibid.*, p. 17.

[7]*Ibid.*, p. 22.

[8]I'm looking at this concept briefly here, but examine it in much greater detail in *Knowing God's Will*, and provide much more biblical basis. See M. Blaine Smith, *Knowing God's Will: Finding Guidance for Personal Decisions* (Downers Grove, Ill.: InterVarsity

Press, 1991), pp. 175-184.

[9]Matthew 5:31-32, 19:3-12; Mark 10:2-12; Luke 16:18.

[10]M. Blaine Smith, *Should I Get Married?* Revised Edition (Downers Grove, Ill.: InterVarsity Press, 2000), pp. 137-156.

[11]Judith Sills, Ph.D., *How to Stop Looking for Someone Perfect and Find Someone to Love* (New York: Ballentine Books, 1985).

[12]I reference some of these articles and include some classic photos from them in an article on my ministry website, "The Shortest Cop on the Force," at www.nehemiahministries.com/shortcop.htm.

[13]Daphne Rose Kingma, *Coming Apart: Why Relationships End and How to Live Through the Ending of Yours* (New York: Fawcett Crest, 1987), p. 71.

[14]Deborah Tannen, *You Just Don't Understand: Women and Men in Conversation* (New York: Harper Paperbacks, 2001).

[15]Debbie Maken: *Getting Serious About Getting Married: Rethinking the Gift of Singleness* (Wheaton, Ill.: Crossway Books, 2006), pp. 166ff.

[16]Ann Gerhart, "I Wanna Say, Just Follow Me," *The Washington Post*, December 6, 2009, p. E9.

[17]Herbert J. Miles, *Singles, Sex and Marriage* (Waco, Tex.: Word, 1983), p. 118.

[18]*Ibid.*, pp. 118-19.

[19]Napoleon Hill, *Think and Grow Rich* (Hollywood: Melvin Powers Wilshire Book Co., 1966), pp. 20-21.

About the Author

BLAINE SMITH, A PRESBYTERIAN PASTOR, SPENT 30 YEARS as director of Nehemiah Ministries, Inc., a resource ministry based in the Washington, D.C. area. He retired the organization in 2009, but continues to use the name Nehemiah Ministries for free-lance work.

His career has included giving seminars and lectures, speaking at conferences, counseling, and writing. He is author of nine books, including *Knowing God's Will* (original and revised editions), *Should I Get Married?* (original and revised editions), *The Yes Anxiety*, *Overcoming Shyness*, *The Optimism Factor*, *One of a Kind*, and *Marry a Friend*, as well as numerous articles (all books except *Marry a Friend* published by InterVarsity Press). These books have been published in more than thirty English language and international editions. He is also lecturer for *Guidance By The Book*, a home study course with audio cassettes produced by the Christian Broadcasting Network as part of their *Living By The Book* series.

Blaine served previously as founder/director of the Sons of Thunder, believed by many to be America's first active Christian rock band, and as assistant pastor of Memorial Presbyterian Church in St. Louis. He is an avid guitarist, and currently performs with the

Newports, an oldies band active in the Washington, D.C. area.

Blaine is a graduate of Georgetown University, and also holds a Master of Divinity from Wesley Theological Seminary and a Doctor of Ministry from Fuller Theological Seminary. He and Evie live in Gaithersburg, Maryland. They've been married since 1973, and have two grown sons, Benjamin and Nathan. Their first grandchild, Jackson Olen, was born to Ben and his wife Lorinda in 2009.

Blaine also authors a twice-monthly online newsletter, *Nehemiah Notes*, featuring a practical article on the Christian faith, posted on his ministry website and available by e-mail for free. You may e-mail Blaine at mbs@nehemiahministries.com.

22539121R00147

Made in the USA
Middletown, DE
02 August 2015